Continued Praise for *Find Your Right Direction: The Israel Gap Year Guide*

Other authors are saying...

"A well-organized, information-packed, and interactive resource. Phyllis Folb's unique history and perspective has given the reader a story-filled, inspirational, and motivating book that delivers an important and powerful message about the Gap Year in Israel."

—**Rae Nelson, *The Gap Year Advantage* by Karl Haigler and Rae Nelson**

"Tens of thousands of students have used the Israel Gap Year to enrich their Jewish knowledge and commitment. With the help of the *Find Your Right Direction: The Israel Gap Year Guide*, many more will follow the same exciting and enlightened path."

—**Michael Medved, nationally syndicated radio talk show host and bestselling author, *God's Hand on America***

"Phyllis Folb leads readers on a VIP tour of the remarkable variety of experiences in Israel for Gap Year students. This is your go-to book to discover how transformative these experiences can be spiritually, intellectually, and personally."

—**Judy Gruen, author, *The Skeptic and the Rabbi: Falling in Love with Faith***

"Phyllis Folb's book is a must read for every Gap Year counselor, prospective student, or parent as it provides the arguments and tools for creating the most informative growth opportunity."

—**Jodi Samuels, author, *Chutzpah, Wisdom and Wine***

"Phyllis Folb speaks with earnestness, intelligence, and respect for what is important about the Israel Gap Year. *Find Your Right Direction: The Israel Gap Year Guide* helps Jewish youth see the merits of this year as bridge between high school and college to finding themselves in the Jewish homeland and people."

—Batya Casper, author, *Israela; Hidden: Nistar;* and *Electra*

Gap Year professionals said...

"Having been to over twenty countries on five continents to promote Israel Gap Year Programs, I can safely say that no one knows the field better than Phyllis Folb. She has a wealth of knowledge, experience, and cares about matching each participant with the perfect program. She herself is the ultimate Israel Gap Year Program resource. In a post-COVID-19 outbreak world this book will be a valuable resource to help everyone looking for an Israel Gap Year Program."

—**Simon Cohen, Co-Founder and Admissions Director of Aardvark Israel Programs**

"Israel is a bigger Gap Year destination than we thought with almost 50% of those polled in GYA 2020 National Alum Survey reporting that they've gone there. What Phyllis Folb is facilitating for young people will change their lives and this book will continue to help raise awareness of the benefits and value of the Gap Year in Israel."

—**Ethan Knight, Executive Director Gap Year Association**

"Phyllis offers an absolute wealth of information on how to plan a productive and meaningful Gap Year in Israel. I have often relied on her expertise in this arena in my work with Gap Year students. With *Find Your Right Direction: The Israel Gap Year Guide,* you too will have Phyllis' knowledge at the ready to help you in the Gap Year research and planning process."

—**Julia Rogers, EnRoute Consulting**

Educators and counselors wrote...

"*Find Your Right Direction: The Israel Gap Year Guide* is a unique book that lets you see the breadth of Israel programs that are available. This is a resource that brings it all together for you."

—Bruce Powell, President Jewish School Management

"Phyllis' knowledge of Israel Gap Year programs is second to none. This resource will provide valuable insight into these exciting options."

—Jim Patterson, Director of the Kutler Center, Harvard-Westlake School

"A much needed resource. I can't wait to promote it with JCHSB families."

—Lauren Cook, Dean of College and Gap Advising,
Jewish Community High School of the Bay

"As the only college counselor for a public high school serving over 1,200 students, it is incredibly important to have up -to-date resources to share with my students. *Find Your Right Direction: The Israel Gap Year Guide* will be a go-to choice when discussing the Israel Gap Year option."

—Casey Rowley, College Counselor, Beverly Hills High School

Parents said...

"We knew the importance of having our daughter spend a Gap Year in Israel after high school graduation, but with so many programs to choose from, we wanted to make sure she found the right fit. Phyllis Folb is so knowledgeable, and has put together a resource that will help every student find the program that will ensure they get the most out of their year. Our daughter grew more in her learning, her love of Israel, and as a person during her Gap Year than any other time in her life. With Phyllis' guidance, your child will too!"

—Shawni Modrell-Astroff, parent of Israel Gap Year alum

The Israel Gap Year Guide

FIND YOUR RIGHT DIRECTION

PHYLLIS FOLB

REDWOOD PUBLISHING, LLC

Printed in the United States of America

Published by Redwood Publishing, LLC
Orange County, California
www.redwooddigitalpublishing.com
info@redwooddigitalpublishing.com

First Printing, 2020

ISBN 978-1-952106-62-0 (paperback)
ISBN 978-1-952106-63-7 (ebook)

Library of Congress Control Number: 2020915248

Disclaimer: This book is designed to provide information and motivation to its readers. It is sold with the understanding that the author and publisher are not engaged to render any type of psychological, legal, or any other kind of professional advice. The content of each article is the sole expression and opinion of its author.

If you would like to order books in bulk directly from the author, at a volume discount, please contact Phyllis Folb at: email: pfolb@findyourrightdirection.com.

For more information about the information laid out in this book, you can also visit:
https://www.americanisraelgapyearassociation.org/

10 9 8 7 6 5 4 3 2 1

Israel Gap Year has come to equal Jewish continuity and legacy.

This book is dedicated to my family whose diversity reminds
me that no matter how you practice the fire of Torah,
Israel and the Jewish People burn bright in all of us.

- *Molly and Lawrence Folb*—The embodiment of gentleness and laughter.
- *Nancy and Jack Fishman*—Who ignited my first interest in Shabbat and traditional Jewish practice.
- *Ruth and Ben Katchen*—Devotion personified.
- *Annie Joseph and Stanley Folb*—Love and inclusiveness that say Tikkun Olam.
- *Edy Lipen*—Pure joy.
- *Ike Lipen*—What duty looks like.
- *Tina Gall and Sheryl Katchen*—Women of valor.
- *Mark*—The Moshe to my Tzipora.
- *Lauren and Julia*—My beloved daughter of G-D and my Bracha whose successful gap years in Israel inspired this book and who with their husbands, Daniel and Shmuel, have built homes instilled with Jewish values and practice that are inspiring the next generation.
- *My ten grandchildren, to date: Temima, Emuna, Bruria, Margalit, Nessia, Odelia, Rayli, Shai, Jordan, and Levi*—the legacy that this book is all about.

CONTENTS

A Daughter's Journey

Almost twenty years ago, my husband Mark and I put our oldest daughter, Lauren, on a flight to begin a Gap Year in Israel. As a recent high school graduate questioning where she wanted to land Jewishly, we were concerned that she would be lost in the college milieu that awaited her. We hoped that the warm blanket of Israel would strengthen her to remain true to Jewish values and to resist pressures to conform that often present themselves on a student's first foray into campus life. Despite her initial protests, we presented Lauren with the "opportunity" to devote a year of study at a program of her choosing in Israel. She chose one known for self-exploration with soft guidance from warm mentorship. The first few weeks of Lauren's Gap Year *were* difficult. At first, my daughter felt so lost in Jerusalem. She was distressed that she could jog through surrounding observant neighborhoods only if dressed modestly in a skirt. She found more comfort in the familiarity of beaches, malls, and restaurants. But then, quietly, without fanfare, the magic took hold—friendships developed, mentors emerged, and the learning jumped off the page into real-life examples of Jewish-connected joy.

When my family and I visited her that January, I met a self-assured young woman, maneuvering easily through the streets of Jerusalem, chatting confidently with shopkeepers and taxi drivers in Hebrew and hosting her friends for get-togethers in our rented apartment. "Mommy, you were so right about coming to Israel." She told me that the highlight of her year had been feeling "comfortable in her own skin."

The highlight of my daughter's Gap Year had been feeling "comfortable in her own skin."

I witnessed a special quality to her demeanor, a distinctive inner glow of growing maturity, self-confidence, and focus with generally more appreciation for her family and heritage.

Her time spent in Israel and her college education were not mutually exclusive. I considered the experience an investment in her soul. My daughter did not defer her education but began a path of continued learning, self-exploration, and spiritual growth that brought her happiness and direction that has helped her navigate her life.

That daughter went on to graduate magna cum laude from Columbia University, founded and now heads an innovative school in Manhattan, and is the mother of six children who are inspired by a mother who is clear and focused in her parental guidance. Lauren's experience, along with my second daughter's successful Gap Year experience, influenced my future professional life as a college counselor and advocate for the Israel Gap Year experience through the American Israel Gap Year Association.

My View as Teen Counselor

Before founding the American Israel Gap Year Association (AIGYA), I worked with teens as a high school counselor. I saw so many students who were on an academic racetrack in high school, and by the time they got to college they were burned out or lacked focus. Students with no real sense of purpose and meaning and no ultimate goal in mind except getting into college. I finally realized that taking the time to breathe and explore who you are culturally, combined with some real-world experience, was not unique to my own children but crucial to a meaningful and successful post-secondary experience.

A meaningful Gap Year allows you to develop a sense of true self-awareness as a catalyst to finding your right direction in college or whatever the next step will be.

The vision of the Gap Year as a deep gorge that you fall into needs to change and be seen more as a bridge to cross over. You are not on hold during a Gap Year. If anything, you are on an ever-evolving trajectory to see what impact you can have on the world. The bridge you cross to new experiences will be built on the educational foundation already provided by parents, educators, and mentors. A meaningful Gap Year allows you to develop a sense of true self-awareness as a catalyst to finding your right direction in college or whatever the next step will be.

Because the Gap Year is *not* a goof year, you are wise to start thinking about it early as a viable option to explore.

So You Want to Take a Gap Year in Israel? Good Idea!

If you picked up this book, then a Gap Year is probably already on your radar. You may be feeling positive about the idea but do not yet know all the Israel Gap Year opportunities there are to explore. If you picked up this book, it's because you are in some way connected to the Jewish people—through family, camp, school, temple, lox and bagels, or some other way. We will show you the many reasons why Israel should be your place of destination for a fantastic Gap Year whether you are exploring your heritage or looking for your career. While I wrote this book with you—the student—in mind, to help you identify the best program to maximize your potential, it can also be read and used by parents, teachers, and counselors helping students to make those choices.

It will give you the vocabulary and resources to have the conversations you need to have about what a Gap Year means and the resources to intelligently make the right choices.

The American Israel Gap Year Association was founded in 2013 to champion Jewish continuity through the Israel Gap Year experience, connecting students with engaging opportunities to study, work, and travel across the denominational spectrum. We are not a Gap Year program unto ourselves, but an umbrella organization that works in concert with programs in Israel and with Jewish high school students and their families to find their right fit. While we don't represent any one particular program, we are a conduit and a resource to many.

The crown jewel of our organization is our incredible ambassador program which selects a diverse group of articulate gappers in a variety of programs to chronicle their year on social media, on our own Instagram page, @IsraelGapYear. We call them ambassadors because they are a connection between AIGYA and the individual Gap Year programs and you! AIGYA Ambassadors' stories and testimonials are woven throughout the book; ninety percent are recently returned alums, while a few are college graduates, who have a longer perspective of time in which to look back at their Gap Year experience. To learn more about the alums, the ambassadors, and AIGYA, check out the videos on our website, www.AIGYA.org.

This book is the product of my years of experience as a high school counselor and as founder of AIGYA. The first part of the book will lay the groundwork of why Israel should be your place of destination, giving you historical context, personal reflection, and some how-to tools to make your evaluation. The second half of the book will provide you with a comprehensive program guide with summary descriptions of all the Gap Year options in Israel and insider tips from recent AIGYA ambassadors about the best things to explore during an Israel Gap Year.

Are you ready to start your journey? I can't wait to share all the possibilities with you!

CHAPTER ONE

Israel, Judaism, the Future, and Me

"Walking out of my apartment every day and stepping on the stone ground that my ancestors fought for not too long ago is an incredible feeling. Jewish history had always felt like just another school subject to me but living here has made it into an integral part of discovering my identity as a Jew in the modern world."

—Yali Miller

Israel—as an ideal as well as a physical place—is central to Judaism. In pre-modern times, hundreds of Jews literally risked their lives to simply walk the streets of Israel as a Jew. Many of these pilgrimages were not made to escape religious persecution or for financial gain, but to follow a deep longing of the heart. *Next Year in Jerusalem,* we say at the end of the Passover Seder. *O Jerusalem,* we sing. Mention of Israel is central to Jewish prayers, from the moment one is named, and at every major life event thereafter. Hatikvah, the Israeli National

Anthem, speaks about the "yearning soul of a Jew" for "the East to Zion."

Yet for centuries, the sheer physical obstacles to travel east to Zion were daunting. During the nearly two thousand years between the destruction of the second temple and the founding of modern Israel in 1948, very many Jews would have been, as Hillel Rabbi Moshe Daniel Levine recently said on a video posted to his Facebook page, "so excited to hear every last detail of Israel, what it means, how it looks. They'd want to know about all the nuances."[1]

Today, in the twenty-first century, you can hop on an airplane and find out for yourself what Israel means, how it looks, and all the nuances. By spending a Gap Year in Israel you are fulfilling a two-thousand-year-old history of Jews' longing for Israel!

The Tradition of Traveling to Israel

Beginning in the 1920s, *tiyul*—hiking trips—were organized by Zionist pioneers who wanted fellow Jews to visit newly established Tel Aviv and, most importantly, to see the land then called Palestine. Youth groups from Europe (where hiking was a popular activity) were especially encouraged to trek the rocky cliff to Masada or the wooded trail to Mount Meron's peak. Local guides led the hikes and imparted information about the country's geology, geography, botany, and more. Educators in the *Yishuv*, the small Palestinian Jewish community that existed before the state of Israel was established, believed that to know the land of Israel would inspire love for the land where Jews had been present for three thousand years.

The Yishuv pioneers knew that to love the land of Israel was to commit to the difficult but deeply satisfying work of rebuilding a home for the Jewish people. As sociologist and Vanderbilt University Professor Shaul Kelner writes in his book, *Tours that Bind: Diaspora,*

Pilgrimage, and Israeli Birthright Tourism, "Tiyul was not so much an act of teaching information about the land of Israel (for which a textbook would have sufficed) as it was an act of sacralizing the homeland—affirming its importance through the ritual of 'knowing' it."[2] Experiencing Israel was—and is—the deepest kind of knowledge.

As AIGYA alum Eli Solomon found, "weekly tiyuls around Israel allowed me to see this beautiful land in ways which you cannot experience by simply reading books or watching videos."

Organized trips for Jewish youth groups to Israel really began to take root and grow in the 1950s, soon after Israel was founded. By then, the experience might also include prayer, study, working on a *kibbutz* (a collective community in Israel that was traditionally based on agriculture, although today, all manners of industry have been added to that model; the kibbutz often combines language immersion and work programs for gappers), and meetings with Israeli teenagers. Much like present-day Gap Year trips, they were intended to strengthen Jewish identity, especially in young American and Canadian Jews. Hiking and sightseeing were still valued, but educators began to recognize how important independent exploration and learning and simply meeting and getting to know each other was to students. The purpose and meaning of traveling to Israel began to be seen much as it is today—a place to connect to new dimensions of yourself as well as to the rich and nuanced history of the Jewish homeland. That may be the reason why, according to a 2017 survey conducted by the Pew Research Center, nearly half of the 6.7 million Jews living in the United States

> *The purpose of traveling to Israel is to connect to new dimensions of yourself as well as to the rich history of the Jewish homeland.*

have traveled to Israel at least once (many have done so more than once).[3]

So—when you spend a Gap Year in Israel, you are connecting to *two thousand* years of Jewish longing, and you are joining a one-hundred-year-old tradition of visiting and experiencing the land!

Ok, So I Know the History of Israel, but What about Today?

Did you know you can pursue just about any interest in Israel?

Fascinated by high-tech? Internships offer hands-on experience with top industry professionals to develop your skills to become a programmer, designer, or app developer. Next to Silicon Valley, Israel has the highest number of high-tech companies in the world. Voicemail, instant messaging, the Waze GPS system, and USB flash drives are all examples of Israeli tech inventions.

Passionate about the arts? A gapper who was a singer and a voice major found an internship in an Arab-Israeli children's choir. Teaching music to kids helped her see that she could be a teacher as well as a performer. Israel has ten film schools, the internationally respected Israeli Philharmonic Orchestra, a long history of supporting the arts, and more museums per capita than anywhere else in the world.

Drawn to religious learning and observance? You know that some of the most revered teachers and best schools to study Torah and other Hebrew texts are located in Israel. There's even the option of attending secular *yeshiva* that's devoid of religious observance and simply geared to the educational study of Jewish texts. Jewish learning is undoubtedly sweeter when undertaken in the holy land itself.

Concerned about the environment? You might not know that Israeli-developed drip irrigation is one of the most valued agricultural innovations of modern times and that Israeli scientists study drought-resistant crops. Working the land, learning about farming, or getting into gardening in a big way can all be pursued.

Is a plant-based lifestyle important to you? Tel Aviv hosts more vegan restaurants than any other place in the world.

Do you think you want to join the military? The Israeli Defense Force (IDF) is one of the finest in the world and joining is often seen as a rite of passage and an incredible honor by Israeli teens. If you are interested, there are some gapper programs that offer a taste of the military life so that you can experience it first, and join when you feel ready.

From fashion to medical internships to volunteering in social services, there is a way for you to become involved in just about anything during your Gap Year.

Fashion, medicine, biology, entrepreneurship, volunteering in social services—you name it and there is a way to become involved during your Gap Year experience. From a single-sex yeshiva to a co-ed agrarian co-op, there's a program for every interest. You can be a secular person and study the rabbinic discussions of the Gemara, or a religious person and study artificial intelligence and machine learning. Israel's small size offers incredible access to whatever you're passionate about as well as the ability to combine several disparate interests into a single Gap Year experience.

A tiny dynamo of a country, Israel is forward-thinking, highly technological, and economically flourishing. For the record, it's the only country in the Middle East that's a proven democracy, is religiously tolerant (recognizing fifteen different religions), holds free and fair elections, and legally protects LGBTQ and women's rights. Generally speaking, Israelis are forthright in an exchange of differing views which makes for lively, thought-provoking discussion and debate.

Been There, Done That, Why Should I Spend a Whole Year in Israel?

Maybe you have already made a short-term visit to Israel with family, school, or camp. Or, maybe you have never set foot on Israeli sand or stone and are planning a short trip there at some point. Spending a week or two in Israel is like a summer romance. By comparison, spending a whole year in Israel allows you to experience the rhythms of daily life and the commitment is like getting engaged. You really get to know the country's breadth and depth. Like any meaningful love relationship, you will see flaws as well as great beauty.

Masa Israel Journey, a joint project between the Israeli government and the Jewish Agency of Israel surveyed nearly six thousand people from over sixty countries who had participated in a program in Israel. In their report, "Lifting The Veil: Report on the Retrospective Study of Alumni: 2005–2014," they found that those who attended longer programs, of eight months or more, reported higher rates of engagement in Jewish life when they went home than the participants who went on short programs.[4] As one Masa alum reflected, "I became involved in the day-to-day life of Israel, learning a language, living amongst people . . . Making a place my home (navigating roads and grocery stores, meeting people . . .) made me feel like I belonged. These are memories that I am still strongly attached to . . . These are deeper experiences and connections that you cannot get on a blitz tour."[5]

Recent AIGYA Ambassador Mia Raskin remembers a sunrise hike on a sandy mountain overlooking the water as the moment when she truly understood the uniqueness of Israel. She also remembers the feeling "like no other" when she walked down Ben Yehuda street and realized she was surrounded by Jewish people. She felt profoundly connected to what she called "a family of strangers" that had her back. "Asking for directions, saying hello in a restaurant or *slicha* [excuse me] after bumping into people on the bus is a connection that you cannot compare to anything in the diaspora [anything outside of Israel]."

Spending four months or more in Israel allows you to clearly see and understand the country in ways that are impossible to do from afar. Whatever your current attachment to Israel, spending a Gap Year—or even part of a year—will be transformative and deepening. As AIGYA Ambassador Oren Rimon said, "I used to think Israel was this place on the other side of the world where a lot of Jews lived, but now I see it as the home of the Jewish people."

Taking Ownership of Your Jewish Identity

In today's world, most high school students have multiple identities—student, athlete, social activist, artist, Jew, and more! The Gap Year intertwines the different elements of your identity into an incredibly rich experience that will speak to you on every level. Not only will you expand your global horizons by spending time in Israel, but you will also be exposed to new ways of looking at history, with personal relevance, and so much more—all through a Jewish lens. This perspective will give you an opportunity to learn more about yourself and to find out what energizes you, what confounds you, what inspires you, and what your passions are.

Perhaps more than any other time in your life, your late teens and early twenties are a time of self-exploration—and that includes religious identity. Too many high school and college students seem afraid to even talk about religion, yet religion is a powerful shaper of who you are. Spiritual development plays a crucial role in becoming an independent adult. Yet, according to the Hillel Foundation, which has its finger on the pulse of collegiate Jewry, most Jewish college students are choosing not to be Jewish. Too many students are running away from or are ashamed of their religion.[6]

A Gap Year gives you an opportunity to learn more about yourself and find out what energizes and inspires you.

This is a crucial time to learn about yourself Jewishly and then decide who you want to be in much the same way as you decide who you want to be socially or academically. A Gap Year gives you the time and space to experience Israel for yourself and experiment with ways of being Jewish that you may not have previously considered. Thoughtful discussions about religion and its place in your life take place alongside conversations about gender, race, and class. Yes, talking about religion can be cool!

No matter how Judaism is present in your family—from the most observant to the most secular—you are now of an age to decide for yourself what kind of Jew you want to be.

- What are your values?
- What is your world view?
- How do you want to live your daily life?

- How do you understand other people?
- What career will you choose?
- How will you raise a family?

AIGYA ambassador Ellie Zisblatt spoke for many when she said that, "learning and living in Jerusalem means experiencing Judaism at its most central place on earth."

All these big and important questions are yours to figure out and going to Israel is the perfect place to do that. Being Jewish in Israel is about history, food, culture, politics, land, language, and religion. It's about late-night falafel runs, bus travel, water sports, visiting the Western Wall, and spending Shabbos with a welcoming Israeli family. "Wherever you choose to go," said Eli Solomon, "know that the Israel Gap Year experience is more than just a break in between high school and college; this year is a chance to grow, meet new friends, learn in a stress free environment."

Going to Israel is the place where you can take ownership of your Jewish identity and create an indelible bond with the Jewish people. A Gap Year in Israel provides the opportunity to dialogue with thoughtful mentors who are outside family influence, and can help guide young people to who they are and where they will go. Such a level of immersion will fortify teens to remain true to Jewish values even if challenged during the college years that lie ahead.

Israel is the only place where Judaism can be fully expressed rather than as a minority religion existing at the margins of another country's majority religion. Israel is a place where Judaism can be lived. You may be surprised at how many different ways there are of being Jewish in Israel. Take, for example, the practice of covering one's head. Whether it be a *kippot* or hat for men or a scarf for women, there are countless ways to express yourself in identification with a specific group and commitment to a way of life. The color, texture, and size of a head covering is almost like a badge of belonging. Choosing not to cover your head is also a way of being Jewish—over forty percent of Israeli Jews identify as secular.

Hebrew University Emeritus Professor Barry Chazan is an authority on contemporary Israel education who cares deeply about what today's young people need and how they best learn about Judaism and Israel. In his 2016 opinion piece, "The Subject of Israel Education is Not Israel," published in *The Times of Israel*, he explained that, "The aim of contemporary Jewish education and life is . . . about enabling a meaningful synergy between Israel, being Jewish and being human. Israel is important because it is connected to being Jewish, and being Jewish is important because it is about making us truly human."[7] Spending a Gap Year in Israel provides a connection between high school and a life-long meaningful synergy between the Jewish homeland, Judaism, and yourself as a human being.

Israel and Your Future

Unfortunately, you are living in a time when anti-Semitism and anti-Zionism are real. College years help to shape identity, but also often pressure teens to challenge the very foundational principles of faith. On college campuses, where anti-Semitism and anti-Zionism is on the rise, students risk being swept up in the momentum of these movements, which often run high on emotion and low on factual reality. Having a strong Jewish identity and a strong attachment to Israel lets you separate the true facts from myths and prejudices. A Gap Year will build your commitment to Israel and the Jewish community, and make you proud to embrace Judaism in whatever form you choose. These are traits you will carry with you throughout your own life and also pass on to younger generations.

During a Gap Year in Israel, you will learn to look beyond the media reports about Israel to discover the reality behind the myths, and to trust your own findings and perceptions in your quest for answers to questions about Israel, Judaism, the world, and yourself. Your first-hand experiences will make you a credible witness. The same Masa Israel Journey study mentioned earlier found that people who spend extended time in Israel are forty-three percent more likely to take a leadership role in Jewish life at home or university. In this way, a Gap Year in Israel empowers you as a young adult to enter college as what we at AIGYA call an "ambassador of truth."

Speaking of college—in case you are wondering, colleges like Gap Year students. A *lot*. That's because they have seen that Gap Year students are more independent, resilient, and responsible than those who go straight to college. There's plenty of evidence indicating that a Gap Year improves academic performance as well, and some programs offer academic credit that will transfer.

Bruce J. Powell, founder and former head of de Toledo High School, Milken Community High School, and General Studies Principal Yeshiva University of Los Angeles High School, has been deeply involved in Jewish education for nearly fifty years. He is an avid supporter of students taking a Gap Year in Israel. "When the students come back from a Gap Year in Israel I have seen a maturity that goes way beyond the single year," Powell said. "They do better in college when they come back, universally. And the clarity that happens during that year in Israel is what transforms them."

Independence, the essence of modern adulthood, relies on developing confidence, competence, and resilience. If a Gap Year gives you experiences that build these traits, a Gap Year in Israel will also answer many of the pressing personal questions to ease you on the path to adulthood. Deciding to do something extraordinary, like a Gap Year, before starting college will allow you the space to grow into a mature, independent individual as you start the next phase of your life. Choosing to spend that year in Israel will build a foundation that will create meaning and connection in today's rapidly changing world. And even more importantly, you will come away from your year in Israel challenged, excited, and inspired to continue your own journey of self-discovery.

Experiencing a Gap Year in Israel will build a foundation that will create meaning and connection in today's rapidly changing world.

This first chapter gave you an overview of the possibilities Israel offers for a Gap Year and the reasons why it can be a crucial chapter in your life. The next chapter will lead you through some self-exploration questions that will help you think about and frame what *you* really want from a Gap Year experience in Israel.

CHAPTER TAKEAWAYS:

- When you spend a Gap Year in Israel, you are connecting to *thousands* of years of Jewish history.
- Spending time in Israel allows you to take ownership of your Jewish identity and your connection to the land and Jewish people.
- You can pursue any interest in Israel and a Gap Year will help you identify your passions, find your strengths, and energize you for the years to come.

CHAPTER TWO

Who Am I?
What Inspires Me?

"To spend a year in Israel is an unimaginable experience and one which I not only recommend, but wholly believe is the most important year in the life of a young Jewish person."

—Eli Solomon

"I learned so much about Israel and even more about myself. I made lifelong friendships and precious memories. My life has completely changed from this experience."

—Sarah Katchen

Your Gap Year: Let's Change Your Visual

Let's create a new visual. Think of this year between high school and college as a bridge rather than a gap because this is the year that you will cross over from what was to what will be.

This journey is a time when you get to discover yourself and one that will make you more successful in the next phase of life. As Yali Miller put it, "I no longer feel that taking a Gap Year is a break before my 'life.' Rather, it's the foundation for my 'life.' Taking a Gap Year in Israel has given and continues to give me incredibly strong confidence in myself, my Judaism, and tools to take on whatever the next chapter of my life may be."

"I no longer feel that taking a Gap Year is a break before my 'life.' It is the foundation for it. A Gap Year has given and continues to give me incredibly strong confidence in myself, my Judaism, and tools to take on whatever comes next."

What do *you* want? How do you see yourself as a young adult? These are essential questions and taking a Gap Year is the optimum way to find your answers.

No doubt you have worked hard to get to where you are now. Whether you have been driven to succeed, felt overwhelmed by academic demands, or both, know that pressure and drive and stress are not sufficient for reaching your life goals. Genuine success is not about how to fill in the right bubbles on an exam or how to play the game to raise your GPA. What's also needed, as an underpinning to all that effort, is self-exploration and the emotional maturity to become energized about your future.

Not a Detour!

Higher education is an investment—one you want to make wisely. You want it to be a place of learning and purpose, and not just the thirteenth year of school. And, sixty thousand dollars or so is a lot of money to spend on a year of college without having a clear purpose or the emotional maturity to make it meaningful. Unfortunately, too many kids go to college without knowing who they are, what they want, or why they are there in the first place. That may be why nearly half—forty-one percent—drop out in their freshmen year and those that continue take an average of six years to graduate from a four-year program. In comparison, students who take a Gap Year graduate from college in four years or less.[8] Their grades skew higher, the majority participate in community services, and eighty-nine percent of those surveyed by the Gap Year Association are satisfied or very satisfied with their jobs. A Gap Year is not a detour!

Even if you're considering a Gap Year, senior year of high school is still the best time to apply to college. That's when you ask teachers for letters of recommendation and talk to guidance counselors about schools that will be a good fit. College applications don't ask if you intend to take a Gap Year. When you accept an offer of admission—usually in the spring of senior year—is when to notify the college that you will defer. Many schools provide a box to check; it's that easy. The college will ask for a deposit, and some admissions counselors may also want to have a general idea of your plans. If you are among the small number of students who re-apply to other schools during your Gap Year you will have plenty of interesting material to include in your personal essay!

A Gap Year is NOT a detour, rather it gives you a roadmap for the year ahead and the years to come.

You do need to plan concurrently for Gap Year and college. That planning will pay off, though, because part of what makes the year magical is that you will have a roadmap for the year ahead.

What Makes Me, Me?

Now that you have evidence and information about its benefits, you still might be wondering how to cross your personal bridge to the next phase of your life. Part of crossing your bridge is figuring out what makes you, you. Figuring that out—a process that will continue to evolve over your lifetime—forms the basis of personal identity, or your sense of self.

For the immediate future, here are some things you need to think about.

What are your goals for the coming year? Maybe you want to learn new things or see new places. Do you want to simply stop, breathe, look around, and recharge? Make new friends? Have an impact on the world? Or are you looking to find a better direction in life? Try writing down your goals. Or talk with your friends, family, and teachers. Any and all of these goals are excellent reasons to give yourself a Gap Year.

When you think about the coming year how do you feel? You might feel overwhelmed with all the choices, curious about what you will experience, excited about an upcoming adventure, anxious about the unknown. Or you might feel that it's no big deal; you'll have some fun and see what happens. It's natural to feel a simultaneous mixture of more than one emotion, or to feel yourself moving between several different emotions. Let your curiosity and excitement move you forward. Don't be put off by feeling anxious. Lots of people are anxious about change, and then they go on to have a fabulous experience.

How do you want to grow? Do you want to become more aware of the world? Do you want to grow spiritually? Become more independent, confident, and emotionally mature? Understand yourself better? The good news is that you will probably grow in most of these ways—and more!—during a Gap Year.

What story do you want to tell your friends and family when the year is over? Maybe you want to keep a photo-journal, blog, or audio record with tales of adventure and stories of the people you meet. Do you want to acquire new perspectives about yourself and the world to share with others? Impress people with your achievements? You may simply feel gratitude for slowing down and becoming energized.

As one gapper said before embarking on a year away, "Going to Israel for the year means seeing who I really want to be for myself, not for my parents, my friends, my teachers; just me." That's true, and it's also true that thinking about these questions will help you chart your course. You may keep finding answers as you plan and continue to gain clarity during your Gap Year. Upon her return from a year away, Yali Miller said, "While I knew I wanted to 'grow' as a person, I didn't completely understand what that meant for me and my life to spend a year doing so. I now know it means creating special connections with mentors who can inspire me, meeting and learning from people every day with completely different views and opinions than me, and being given opportunities to do good in the community." Max Levin, who has now graduated college remembers that, "When I came back from my Gap Year, I had a clear sense of direction and focus, and I knew how to apply myself in college."

> *A Gap Year can help you understand what growth truly means.*
>
> *It's about forging special connections to people who inspire you, learning from people with different views and opinions than your own, and getting the opportunity to do good.*

Your Newfound Independence

Becoming an independent adult is about developing confidence, competency, and resilience. A Gap Year in Israel allows you to do all three by giving you the freedom to do more things on your own and develop more responsibility for yourself.

Yali Miller had this piece of advice: "Regardless of where you go—college, Israel—there are going to be challenges and there are going to be things that you have to work through. But there's something about being totally across the world from everything that you're comfortable with and forced to jump in full force and to expose yourself to not only the challenges of living on your own and meeting new people but also living in a different country with a different language. And every single day you learn something new. You learn about culture. You learn something new about life, and about taking care of yourself—and that is a responsibility you can take anywhere you go."

If parents have been making the decisions about your day-to-day life, a Gap Year is all about learning to make those decisions for yourself in the company of like-minded friends and caring adults. You too will have the opportunity to cook your own food and do your own laundry. You'll learn how to budget your money, and how to take the bus to find your way around the city or wherever you need to go. You'll take calculated risks; you will make some mistakes and not-so-great choices, but that's part of the process (and makes for good stories!). True confidence comes from knowing you can solve the problems you encounter in your life.

A Gap Year gives you room to become more independent in your thinking as well as in the activities of your daily life. Your brain is very alive at this time in your life; it's basically a well-oiled learning machine that can both absorb new information and really begin to "think about thinking." It's a time to reflect on the big questions you may have about justice, love, meaning, purpose, and G-d. At the same time, your brain is still developing, which is why the experiences you have at this age will partially shape future adult decisions. Engaging with the world in Israel strengthens Jewish values and beliefs about the big questions in life, and that's a worldview you can take anywhere you go.

What Inspires Me?

Gap Year advisors agree that it's crucial that you—the student—choose the kind of Gap Year you want to undertake. Parents and teachers are important advisors, whose input should be addressed and evaluated. But you need to take ownership of what you will do. A Gap Year is the perfect occasion to really get in touch with what inspires you or to try something new that you've always wanted to do. Are you especially drawn to social justice work? Technology? The arts? New places and cultures? Make a list of the things you find inspiring. Then spend a week noticing the little moments that excite and satisfy you. Learning from a smart and caring teacher? Being with friends? Getting immersed in an art project? Writing code? The point is to figure out what's right for *you*.

Another way to think about inspiration is to focus on Israel and Judaism. Are you excited about seeing the land? Learning its history? Studying ancient texts? Maybe you are most interested in simply experiencing what it's like to live like an Israeli. Rory Myerson found that "being in Israel for the trio of holidays in the beginning of the year was so surreal; I felt as if my past holiday celebrations were just a build up to this moment when I experienced the holidays at their max and in the purest form." Eli Solomon found it inspiring (and revelatory) to visit Israeli families in their homes for Shabbat dinners. "I have eaten meals at countless family homes, ranging from places in

Nachlaot to Kiryat Belz. This is one of the main ways to learn about how the Jewish people in Israel live, and also gives you an insight into how radically different some people are despite the fact that we all call ourselves Jewish."

Educational consultant and psychologist Sara Persha believes, "passion is not known until you practice and experience something—otherwise passion is shallow and self-serving." Inspiration is about feeling and passion. Taking this time to find yourself in a new place with new people will help you connect to your deepest passion. Many adults wait until their fifties—or even later—to find out who they are, what motivates them, and the things that inspire them. You have the opportunity to do that now.

What Experiences Do I Want to Have?

Authentic experiences are not the same as busy activities undertaken to add to your college application. Learning via authentic experiences is about rolling up your sleeves and becoming transformed through concrete experiences outside of the classroom, in the world. Hands-on, experiential learning as a supplement to academic learning has been valued for decades. Albert Einstein is famous for having said "learning is experience. Everything else is just information." Central to the idea of experiential learning is reflecting on what you've done. That's why many students choose to keep a journal during their often event-filled year.

Talia Paknoosh's Gap Year included a service-oriented program in which she cared for foster kids. She said that the program taught her "how to be patient and understanding," and that it really opened her eyes "to be grateful for the things and the opportunities" she received in life. Patience, understanding, and gratitude are important emotions you can't learn in the classroom! In keeping with Judaism's tradition of *chesed, or* good deeds, she also volunteered at the Lone Soldier center in Jerusalem where she helped soldiers who did not have family in Israel.

Authentic experiences lead to more authentic experiences. They leave a lasting impact. That was the case for Gila Gordon, who felt all through high school that she wanted to help the world in some way, "but didn't feel the push." Then in Israel she heard a speaker who was raising money to help communities in Africa have running water. Because of the transformative experience she had in Israel this gapper now plans to spend a semester in Africa teaching English.

Jewish studies. Of course, one of the most authentic and unique experiences you can have in Israel is Jewish studies. There are so many programs that welcome Gap Year students that you can certainly find the one that feels right to you. Jewish studies is one of the main reasons that people from around the world, including gappers, choose to go to Israel. Some of the most brilliant scholars and teachers are to be found there; many hold mentoring young adults central to their heart.

Ritual is perhaps the ultimate experience, which is one of the reasons it has endured for centuries. Judaism has always been a lived religion and studying the laws behind its rituals can make you truly appreciative. In truth, the mitzvahs are not rules made up by a bunch of old men long ago but wise experiential practices to make you more powerful, competent, and fulfilled. You might think that lighting candles on Shabbat is an obligation, but if you understand and live the history and intent, it's also a time to have a personal conversation and powerful connection with G-d. "Learning why we follow certain laws and the beauty of mitzvot," said Ariella Benaim, "adds meaning to our everyday lives."

Jewish studies is also fun, and a way to make new friends, some-times lifelong. "Every single student in my school is not only friendly but approachable and committed to growing in their own way in a judgement-free environment," Eli Solomon said. "In the short time I've been in Israel, strangers have become close friends whom I've had late night conversations with, went to far flung places with, and have told countless jokes to."

Perhaps most important, students who go on a Gap Year find that authentic, real world experience gives them a sense of purpose and direction. One gapper graduated high school knowing he wanted to study science, but didn't know why or what he wanted to investigate. During his Gap Year he learned about Israeli farming innovations, such as drip-irrigation and crop preservation. With that acquired perspective, he figured out that he wanted to work on agricultural science. He began college having found his right direction, which influenced the classes he signed up for.

> *Students who go on a Gap Year find that authentic, real world experience gives them a sense of purpose and direction.*

Not everyone returns from a Gap Year with a laser-focus for their major, but the majority build authentic college experiences from their recent Gap Year experiences. Max Levin admitted that, "In high school, I didn't get the best grades, but using the experiences and confidence and discipline from a Gap Year opened up a lot of doors and I somehow ended up at a top-tier school where I was really motivated to learn. Being in Israel wasn't always the easiest time but it built character." Another gapper discovered that she was a political person who felt best working for the greater good. College then became an intellectual proposition and a place where she could learn what she needed to support her right direction in life.

Whatever you choose to do on your Gap Year in Israel you will be experiencing it through a Jewish lens. Your values will be shaped, your confidence strengthened, your history solidified. Whatever profession or path in life you choose going forward will be with this lens. You will be fortified to remain true to Jewish values, making it easier to resist pressure to conform should you be faced with challenges in the future.

The next chapter will help you choose the right program for you.

To get you started, this questionnaire from The Canadian Gap Association may clarify things about yourself and what you want out of a Gap Year. Below is some space after each question so that you can write down your answers as you go, and also any additional thoughts you may have.

Gap Year Quiz

What is your top goal for the Gap Year?
   a.   To learn new things.
   b.   To recharge batteries.
   c.   To see the world.
   d.   To get better direction for my life.

_____

_____

_____

_____

When you think about the upcoming year, how do you feel?
   a.   Overwhelmed
   b.   Curious
   c.   Excited
   d.   Anxious
   e.   Realistic

_____

_____

_____

_____

How do you make decisions?
   a. I make lists and charts.
   b. I follow my heart.
   c. I rely on opinions of others.
   d. I like to choose things I know I will be successful at or that I can make a meaningful contribution to.

_____

_____

_____

_____

What's your best quality?
   a. Optimism
   b. Empathy
   c. Curiosity
   d. My ability to try new things
   e. Personable and friendly
   f. Self-awareness

_____

_____

_____

_____

In what areas do you need to see the most growth?
   a. More confidence.
   b. More worldly.
   c. Better able to communicate.
   d. Better able to budget finances and time.
   e. To understand what I want to do later in life.

_____

_____

_____

_____

You're sitting down with your buddies at the end of your Gap Year. What do you want to say?
   a. Tales of adventure.
   b. Stories of people I met.
   c. Sharing new perspectives.
   d. Gratitude for slowing down and feeling energized.
   e. Tales of achievement.

_____

_____

_____

_____

Use this space to jot down any additional thoughts you have about your prospective Gap Year. What does your ideal Gap Year entail? Is there anything that is very important for you to accomplish during your Gap Year?

_____

_____

_____

_____

_____

_____

_____

_____

_____

_____

_____

_____

_____

_____

_____

_____

_____

_____

CHAPTER TAKEAWAYS:

- A Gap Year is not a detour—in fact, it can help you go to college with a confidence in who you are and a focus to achieve your educational goals.
- Going on a Gap Year may be your first taste of independence, allowing you to develop the tools needed to make your own decisions to govern your own life.
- Learn to be true to your Jewish values and resist the ability to conform when challenged.

CHAPTER THREE

Where Do I Want to Go?

"Being around so many people looking to grow you realize that there are so many unknowns to look into and explore. You have potential you didn't even know existed until you found yourself in a new environment."

—Mia Raskin

"Making new friends, trying new activities and foods and learning to navigate a new country has given me a sense of responsibility and thrill that I've never had before!"

—Ellie Zisblatt

Crossing the Bridge

Now that you have a better idea of your goals and what inspires you, the next step is to find *your* right place for a Gap Year in Israel! This chapter zeroes in on some of the more practical items—structure, travel, work, and independence—to think about in preparing for a meaningful, memorable, and transformative experience as you cross the bridge from high school student to young adult. The chapter also discusses some of the practical concerns that are particular to a Gap Year in Israel such as the location you choose as a home base, opportunities for Jewish studies, and the Jewish holidays.

> *When preparing for a meaningful Gap Year, you'll have to consider things like program structure, whether or not you want to travel, how you want to take classes, and what type of work you want to do.*

Structure

A Gap Year is a well-planned operation that's geared to who you are and who you will become; it will harness passions and inspirations. When looking at and deciding which program to attend, think about what kind of structure you are most comfortable in. Do you love meeting a lot of people? Or do you feel more secure getting to know fewer people well in a small group? Do you want to work closely with a mentor? How much free time do you need?

Knowing the kind of structure your program runs on and how you fit into that structure is important to making your Gap Year a successful experience. Do you function better when you know exactly what classes you'll be taking, or do you want to choose your own classes? Some programs have one curriculum that everyone follows, but many have a huge array of classes from which you can choose. In some programs, all classes take place in the morning, so if you're not a morning person you'll want a program with more flexibility around scheduling.

You need a program with goals, one that will allow you to feel accomplished and confident. Writing down some of the goals you want for yourself is helpful. Then don't be shy about asking both representatives and alums if your goals match with the program's mission.

Focused Learning

Although your first thoughts about a Gap Year may be that learning is off the table, in fact, focused learning is very much part of this year. Focus is an important part of adulthood and knowing who you are helps to find your particular focus. Your Gap Year should include something that you want to zero in on personally, but should also include self-growth, spiritual awareness, academic achievement, or a combination of all three. Unlike high school, where most courses are required, Gap Year classes usually offer a lot of choice. You want to be engaged in whatever and however you learn; be that text-based, partner-style, or experiential. Keep in mind that hands-on internships exist in high-tech companies, advertising firms, fashion houses, and hospitals, all of which will provide insight into possible careers. Some courses at your program may be accepted for credit by your home college. Other courses offer career training, or skills-based instruction in vocations such as teaching, cooking, hair dressing, or participation in emergency medicine with the Israel ambulance service. There is a lot of room for exploration!

Self-growth takes many forms. Some students find that living away from home and with other people is a profound learning experience. Finding personal resiliency when faced with the unexpected is also a form of self-growth. For Sarah Pape, an important part of her Gap Year was "learning how to deal with new situations and drastic change." Self-growth often springs from the people you are around and the relationships you form. As Sarah found, "I couldn't have done it without an incredible support system of friends and staff. We did everything together."

If you attended Jewish day schools, a Gap Year can be a time to make the academic learning really come alive. If you did not have an extensive Jewish education, this is an opportunity to explore and gain confidence in the beauty of Jewish life and observance, a time to claim ownership of a central part of your identity. You don't know what you don't know yet. For Ellie Zisblatt, "the overall environment of the country exudes a different level of spirituality." A Gap Year in Israel is a perfect time to explore your own spiritual awareness.

Israel offers a range of academic opportunities. You can attend an *Ulpan*, a language school, and attend classes at Israeli universities. Or you may want to participate in Israel's unparalleled opportunities to study Jewish texts. "The great thing about my school is that everyone fits in," said Eli Solomon. "No matter if you were Sabbath observant or kosher before you arrived or if you went to a Jewish high school or public school, everyone is treated as an equal and seeks to grow in his own way." About the classes, Eli said that they were "not only enjoyable but tapped into a method of thinking which I have never been exposed to before." Gila Gordon was inspired by, "a vast course selection, from introspective reading to academic type classes that engaged my comfort zone but also challenged me to grow spiritually." Ellie Zisblatt found that, "the idea of this extensive all-day learning seemed daunting to me at first, but it has

"No matter if you were Sabbath observant or Kosher before you arrived or if you went to a Jewish high school or public school, everyone is treated as an equal and seeks to grow in his own way."

truly connected me to my family, ancestors, and the land around me in an unparalleled way."

Travel

Not only will you travel from your home to Israel, but a complete Gap Year includes traveling within the country. Trips—*tuyel*—are the foundation of Israel exploration. The pioneers used extensive travel and hikes through the land to internalize its importance to new residents. Whether you go to the Masada fortress, the desert in Eilat, or the waterfall at Ein Gedi, these time-honored experiences will build the richness of the land, the history, and the people into your soul.

Some programs offer weekly field trips or feature one or two extensive trips during the year; gappers find them rewarding and exciting. "One of the highlights of my Gap Year," said Talia Abel, "was the three-day trip to the desert. We swam in the Dead Sea, spent the night in a Bedouin tent, and saw the border where Israel touches Jordan. It was amazing to travel for such a short time and see how drastically the landscape changes." Eliana Cohen said that travel made her realize "the diversity of people who live in what we call the Israel homeland."

Work

An effective Gap Year involves paid or unpaid work. Most programs will involve some kind of *chesed* (good deeds), and some programs center around service-based learning as the main part of your day. Programs may affiliate with an organized institution such as a hospital or daycare or connect you to local families who need help with, for example, childcare. Gappers have done *chesed* at old-age homes, foster care programs, battered women's shelters, army programs, kibbutz farms or businesses, a horse-therapy program, and even clown training for children's hospital wards.

While getting a work visa is complicated, informal ways to make money exist. Some programs allow for a minimal amount of paid work, such as babysitting, tutoring, doing laundry, or working in the kitchen. If you will need to make money during your stay, you will have to innovate. One gapper earned spending money by serving up a special 11:00 p.m. pasta dish in the kitchen for the others in his program who wanted a late-night snack.

Independence—with Limits!

A Gap Year is about becoming more independent, but you will still be expected to abide by the restrictions of your program. For example, if you are living in a dorm, you may be free to go out in the evenings but required to return by midnight. In Israel, the drinking age is eighteen but that doesn't give you a free ticket to drink irresponsibly, if at all. Most students appreciate the balance between freedom and supervision.

In college, unless you're living on campus in a dorm that has an advisor living there to watch after the residents, you are pretty much on your own. But, in a Gap Year program, you have people looking out for you while still giving you your freedom. That said, rules exist to create a specific type of community for you and the others that live there.

Before you apply to a program, find out what kind of behavior is expected. Don't swim upstream—don't put yourself in a situation where you won't be able to respect the rules and responsibilities. Wherever you go, remember that safety and security rules must be respected one hundred percent.

Ingredients for a Meaningful Gap Year in Israel

Location

"What's so awesome," said Mia Raskin, "is that without even trying you learn so much about yourself and grow naturally from your surroundings." Location does play a role in your experience. The program's location will be your base while in Israel, a kind of second classroom where you get to know the shopkeepers and local neighborhood and where the sights and sounds of the landscape will become familiar. Do you get energized or overwhelmed by the city? Do you need to be closer to nature and the outdoors? Do you want to be near the water?

Programs are located all over the country, so try not to make snap judgements about whether or not you might like a place without doing some research first. Ask other students who might have lived in a specific location and visit travel sites on the Internet and Google maps. Jerusalem, which has a reputation as a spiritual center with a tremendous history (including mosques and churches), also has plenty of hip and wonderful things to do. Tel Aviv, which has a reputation as more secular and urban also has religious communities. Consider also such interesting places as Beersheva, Modiin, or Haifa. The cities have dynamic, heterogenous populations, while some of the smaller places have unique geographical features, cultures, and populations.

Mentors

Because this year is one of exploration, don't underestimate the importance of good guidance, whether from a teacher, counselor, or tour guide. Talia Paknoosh admired that her teachers "made every student feel comfortable and encouraged us every day to break out and push to discover new things about ourselves." Ariella Benaim was grateful that her "very learned teachers not only taught but cared for each and every one of their students far more than we could have expected." Leora Lalezari pointed to her teachers as one of the most important aspects of her time in Israel: "Something I did not realize I would get is the amazing role models; they are the people I have gained the most from. I have learned so much from my teachers inside the classroom but there is so much I have learned from them outside the classroom, the way they act with their family, their husbands/wives, and their children."

Your Gap Year can be largely influenced by things like location, access to (and types of) mentors, and how you experience Shabbat. Make sure to research all of this when reviewing your potential programs.

See if you can arrange to talk to alums or some of the teachers at the programs to get a sense of their student–teacher relationships.

Shabbat and Holidays

Shabbat and the annual cycle of Jewish holidays are foundational to Jewish life and Israeli society regardless of how religious you are or are not. Some programs want you to experience a combination of in-house Shabbats, your own observance in a dorm or apartment, and travel to other people's homes. Leora Lalezari found that "there is so much to learn from going to teachers' homes for Friday night meals and helping them or hanging out with their kids. The way they interact with their families has truly inspired me." Gila Gordon also relished Shabbos at her teachers' houses, especially because it allowed her to experience "each of their communities." During Yom Kippur,

Talia Abel was "amazed how everyone wore white and the streets were empty of cars."

Experiencing many different types of Shabbat and holiday practice is another unique part of a Gap Year in Israel; the varied practices can inform how *you* eventually choose to observe.

Choosing Your Right Program

Note that most programs in this book are for an academic year, but some do let you enroll for one semester or are indeed a half a year. My recommendation is that if at all possible, you take the entire year, even if you decide to do more than one thing, programmatically or personally. If your program is only one semester, you will be able to find other activities that allow you to stay the full year in Israel. Find an internship, work on a kibbutz, create a job for yourself, or travel independently. Utilizing all that time will make you stronger. Bear in mind that everyone goes through an adjustment period when they begin their Gap Year, so you want to make sure you can take full advantage of what comes next, when you truly feel comfortable and at home. This is your year to explore—don't cut it short if you don't have to.

A Collaborative Decision

Ultimately, you will choose a program jointly with your parents, teachers, and mentors—all of whom know you well and have your best interests at heart. Use their insights, along with your foundational principles and education, to help make your decision. The adults will value your decision if it comes from a thoughtful place and mutual dialogue.

Parents, here's one father's description of the decision-making process: "Of course, as a parent, I had in mind what I thought was best for my son. But after speaking with the program representative, my son realized that the place I had in mind wasn't the right place for him. On the flip side, my son had assumed another program was the best one, but it was not right for our family. Fortunately, through our research and discussion, we found a program we both agreed was a great fit. The process was an important bonding experience for us both."

Your Right Direction

Use this time to plan to thoroughly explore your horizon. It may be tempting to cut short the decision-making process if you think you've found the one perfect dream-come-true program but give yourself the proper time to sit with your choices and consider everything before pulling the trigger. You may be surprised to find that there will likely be more than one place that can satisfy your requirements and where you'll be happy! In fact, you will probably apply to three to five possible programs, and once you find out where you are accepted, you will choose the one that feels right.

Note that the classes you take at the universities are not part of an official degree program, even though you may be in a class with regularly enrolled college students. In many cases, your home college may give you credit for your Gap Year coursework by, for example, allowing you to test out of lower level requirements. If, during your Gap Year, you realize that you'd prefer to officially enroll in college in Israel, there are many colleges that take foreign students, but the application is a separate process. Many of the actual Gap Year programs have separate learning opportunities where you can earn vocational certificates, as mentioned earlier.

Questions to Ask Gap Year Program Representatives

Below are some questions to ask Gap Year program representatives. The boldface headings are major topics to cover, and the bulleted questions are prompts to get you started. Use this book like a workbook when you begin to talk to any of the Gap Year representatives. We have provided space below each question for you to write down notes from those conversations, as well as blank space to write additional questions that you may have.

1. What makes your program unique? What's your philosophical approach? What do you consider your mandate, keystone, or hallmark feature?

- Is it a language-based program?
- What kind of Jewish learning is included?
- Does it partner with a university for college classes?
- Is the curriculum experiential?
- What kind of volunteer opportunities are offered?
- Does it offer opportunities for a career track or specific training?

_____

_____

_____

_____

2. Location

- Is the program located in a city or a rural environment? In what part of Israel?

- Are there things to do nearby: markets, restaurants, cultural activities?
- How available is transportation?
- What are the unique features of the location?

_____

_____

_____

_____

3. Trips

- What trips are built into the program schedule?
- Does the program offer international trips?
- Are you given time off to travel independently?

_____

_____

_____

_____

4. How do you describe your learning approach?

- What is a typical day like?
- Is it half or full day learning?
- Are night classes offered?
- Is the schedule formalized or do students choose which classes to take?
- Is the learning mostly text-based, lectures, or partner-style?

_____

_____

_____

_____

5. How would you describe the academic level and workload?
- Are there different levels of learning?
- Is there homework?
- Does it offer college credit?
- Is knowledge of Hebrew required and if so, how much?

_____

_____

_____

_____

6. What kinds of students thrive at your program?
- Does the school cater to kids who need a lot of support?
- Does the school include mostly self-directed and highly motivated students?

_____

_____

_____

_____

7. What are the demographics of the student body?
- Are the students mainly from the U.S.? From the east coast or west coast? Or all over?
- Does the program include international students? Which countries?
- Are most students from day schools or do they also include public schoolers and homeschoolers?

- Is it a diverse community in terms of religious observance or political orientation?
- How many students typically enroll?

---

8. Faculty, mentors, counselors, and staff?

- Who will be the advisors and mentors?
- Are students taught by rabbis, certified educators, men, or women?
- Are there traditional office hours?
- Is there peer-to-peer learning?
- Are recent alums part of the teaching or mentoring?
- Is staff available outside of regularly programmed activities? Home hospitality? Trips?
- Are designated go-to families available? House mothers and fathers?

---

9. What support services are available?

- Are there academic advisors and tutors?
- Are guidance counselors accessible for personal challenges or adjustments?
- What's the access to a nurse or medical care?

_____

_____

_____

_____

10. Where do students go after the Gap Year?

- Do most students go to college?
- Do students pursue continued learning back home or in Israel?
- Do any students go to the army?
- Do students make Aliyah?

_____

_____

_____

_____

11. Shabbat and Holidays

- Are Shabbat and holidays celebrated as part of program activities?
- Does the program arrange for visits to Israeli families in their homes for Shabbat or other holidays?
- Does the program stay open for Sukkot and Passover? Will housing be available?

_____

_____

_____

_____

12. What are the housing options?

- Do most students live in dorms? Apartments?
- How many students live together in a dorm room or apartment?
- Are there apartments with kosher kitchens?
- Is housing part of tuition?
- Is it an actual campus or is the school integrated into the local community?
- How far to the nearest bus stop?
- Is WiFi provided?
- Is there a sports/fitness center available on site? A yard? Does the program have partnerships with local gyms or fitness centers?

_____

_____

_____

_____

13. Meals

- Are meals supplied as part of the tuition? How many?
- Is there a cafeteria?
- Does the program have partnerships with local food providers?
- Is there a food stipend?
- Are kosher meals supplied or available through the program?

_____

_____

_____

_____

14. Rules and Responsibilities

- Are there rules around drinking, partying, and dating?
- Is there a dress code?
- A curfew?
- Is class attendance mandatory?
- What are the safety rules?

_____

_____

_____

_____

We hope this gives you more food for thought. As you peruse the programs in the next section you can make copies of this questionnaire to use as a guide, or you may want to create a spreadsheet to enter information and compare the programs that interest you.

Use the below space to write down additional thoughts from your conversations with Gap Year representatives.

CHAPTER TAKEAWAYS:

- Once you decide to go on a Gap Year, don't forget to also consider the practical side of it (program structure, type of work, etc.).
- Don't rush the decision-making process when selecting your program.
- Talk to as many alums and Gap Year representatives as you can so that you get both focused opinions as well as learn the logistics of your desired program.

CHAPTER FOUR

Program Guide

N ow begins the program descriptions. There are over sixty programs to explore in this guide. What's listed here are mere thumbnail sketches of what each program has to offer. You owe it to yourself to take the next step: visit the programs' website and contact the staff and alums to really make assessments of what is the right direction for you. You should also confirm current cost and start dates.

The guide is arranged very simply. The programs are divided into three broad sections: Co-Ed, Women's, and Men's. Within each section are programs that have academic, religious, travel, and internship opportunities. So don't assume that if you are looking at a co-ed program you won't get the spiritual growth you are looking for or that a single gender program that is typically thought of as "more" religious doesn't offer some high-tech internship or exotic travel.

Keep an open mind, review your lists of thoughts and questions, and enjoy the journey. Revisit your answers to the questions posed earlier in this book so that they are top of mind as you begin to dive into the various programs and their offers. *What are you expecting to get out of a Gap Year? What are specific goals you have in mind for your Gap Year and the years to follow? What is important to you to accomplish during this year?*

After you review these programs, be sure to look at the Resource Page, which will give you contact information for travel, safety, and health issues.

CO-ED PROGRAMS

AARDVARK ISRAEL

www.aardvarkisrael.com
info@aardvarkisrael.com • 646-844-7784
whatsapp: +972-52-429-3681

Description of Program:

Aardvark Israel provides each student with a custom, curated experience designed to advance his or her goals for their Gap Year in Israel. Students live together in apartments in downtown Jerusalem and Tel Aviv, buffer their resumes with ambitious internships, explore their passions through volunteering, learn Hebrew and other fascinating subjects, and receive up to a year of college credit—all while deepening their relationship with Israel, Judaism, and themselves. The program will offer students the opportunity to learn valuable life skills as they live independently with young Jewish students from all over the world. Students can customize their experience further with special interest add-ons and international trips to different countries around the world. Aardvark provides our students with a balanced structure enabling them to build their resume, have meaningful experiences and enough free time to make their own plans to enjoy Israel.

Length of Program:

4 or 9 months

Location of Program:

Tel Aviv and Jerusalem

Supervision:

Program counselors (madrichim) and senior staff members. The ratio of madrichim to students is approximately 1:12.

AARDVARK ISRAEL

(Continued)

Cost Range:

$12,740 to $21,490 for the core program, which can increase dependent upon add-on's. The price of Aardvark Israel includes program tuition, housing, medical insurance, fees for all academic courses, field trips, seminars, local transportation, and more. Each special interest program price includes the cost of all instruction, extra-curricular activities, workshops, and seminars. The World Travel and Aardvark International program prices include round-trip airfare between Israel and the foreign destination and all program costs associated with each trip, including meals during foreign travel.

- **What are living arrangements like:** Fully furnished apartments
- **# of Meals:** Meals are not included in tuition
- **Any other activities or accommodations included in cost:** Social activities and weekend activities
- **Additional add on (that can affect cost):** Sea sports, Aardvark Extreme, Selah (Jewish enrichment), MADA (Israeli Ambulances), Marva (basic training in Israeli Army), and Entrepreneurship. Plus international add-on trips to Spain, Czech Republic, China, Ethiopia, Italy, Germany and Poland and a Nepal Cultural Exchange Program

Religious Observance and/or Program Philosophy:

Inclusive program, all views of Judaism are welcomed. Shomer Shabbat and kosher apartments are available.

AARDVARK ISRAEL

(Continued)

Program Highlights:

- International student population—students have come on our program from over thirty countries and six continents
- Perfect balance between structure and free time
- Resume building internships

Student Highlights:

"Coming on Aardvark has been character building to say the least. There are endless opportunities to surround yourself with stimulation, whether you want to engage in the political, cultural, or religious aspects of Israel. As comforting as it is to stay in bed all day, you are going to want to remember this experience as a time of fulfilment and lots of adventure. So just push yourself because I promise you it is worth it!"

—Rachy

"I think where Aardvark shines is giving students a unique opportunity to just live here. It's getting to know your neighbors on the other balcony, ordering food in Hebrew and not being responded to in English, understanding the angst of a fourth election, and hearing from Israeli right- and left-wingers. It's lunchtimes at work and casual conversations with your boss that reveal the true nature of what lies below the surface of this complicated society. The day-to-day freedom I have had, enriched with classes, trips, and lifelong connections is what has made this experience so deep and unforgettable."

—Ben

"To future Aardvarkians, take every opportunity you can get. Step out of your comfort zone; I know it's cliché but those are the experiences you'll remember the most. Choose a volunteering or interning experience that makes you nervous. Being in a position of unfamiliarity is not always negative – it's where you become independent and learn the most. I was close to bailing on my internship for at risk youth before I even started because I was so nervous—I didn't speak Hebrew, I didn't know how to get there by myself, I was walking into something that was so unfamiliar and scary. But being in that situation has taught me so much more than while I've been in 'comfortable' and 'safe' environments. Also, find time to be with everyone on the program. Everybody I've met is so special and overall, they are the reason my year has been so special. I have lifelong friendships in every part of the globe. I'm so grateful for the year I've had so far."

 —Sarah

ARTZI

artzigap.org • https://www.artzigap.org/copy-of-apply

Description of Program:

Artzi Gap Year program is for American, European young adults who are committed to a creative genre of dance, music, theater, or visual arts, and want to be immersed in the life of a rich and diverse country, while learning about Judaism and connecting to their Jewish identity in an eye-opening and enlightening manner. We create an environment in which the students have the freedom to express themselves, utilize their artistic talents, fall in love with the land, and nurture a lifelong connection with the people and state of Israel (outside the American bubble). Artzi is an all-encompassing program filled with high level courses, trips, volunteer opportunities, communal activities, an internship program, and fun unique experiences, which connects Jewish students from around the world, while promoting core values of the Arts, Israel, and Judaism.

Length of Program:

5 to 9 months

Location of Program:

Kibbutz Bachan near Netanya

Supervision:

Please contact for more details

Cost Range:

$16,500 to $26,000, includes food, accommodations, health insurance, and travel

- **What are living arrangements like:** Students will be living in local apartments. The dorms are equipped with kitchens, bathrooms, a laundry machine, and a communal area.
- **# of Meals:** Three meals a day are provided and all food is strictly kosher. We offer vegetarian and gluten free options as well.
- **Any other activities or accommodations included in cost:** Our tuition includes full healthcare coverage with great English-speaking doctors and 24/7 on call emergency centers. Please contact for more details.
- **Additional add on (that can affect cost):** Personal travel

Religious Observance and/or Program Philosophy

Pluralistic

Program Highlights

- Art mentorship program
- Israel and Judaism
- Volunteering

Student Highlights:

- "My best year ever."
- "First time I learned the deep side of Israel."
- "I found my best friends at the program."

BIG IDEA GAP YEAR @ AARDVARK ISRAEL

https://aardvarkisrael.com/tech-track/
info@aardvarkisrael.com
USA: 646-844-7784 • Whatsapp: +972-52-429-3681

Description of Program:

BIG IDEA @ Aardvark Israel provides participants intensive hi-tech training, professional internships, and a one-of-a-kind Startup Nation experience! It is the ideal choice for anyone looking to boost their career in technology while also having an immersive, educational experience in Israel. During the first semester students will be immersed in a hands-on technology course in Jerusalem to become a front-end developer, earning official developer certification. Continuing to Tel Aviv in the second semester, students will intern alongside Israelis at leading startups.

Participants will also go on weekly field trips around Israel, can earn up to twenty-one university credits in Hebrew and other relevant electives, participate in extracurricular activities, and more! One of the highlights of the program will be in January when students participate in "Impact Month"—a month-long hackathon to design an app for a non-profit organization in Tel Aviv; this is an opportunity to use the skills learned to make a different for a community in need.

Length of Program:

- *September to December:* 4 months in Jerusalem including the coding course
- *September to January:* 5 months (4 months in Jerusalem + 1 IMPACT month)
- *September to May:* 9 months (4 months in Jerusalem, 1 IMPACT MONTH and 4 months interning in Tel Aviv)

BIG IDEA GAP YEAR @ AARDVARK ISRAEL

(Continued)

Location of Program:

Depends which track you choose:
> *Semester*: Jerusalem
> *Semester + IMPACT month*: Jerusalem + Tel Aviv
> *Full year experience:* Jerusalem and Tel Aviv

Supervision:

Approximately one counselor to every fifteen students, plus supporting senior staff

Cost Range:

4 months: $15,490
5 months: $17,990
9 months: $26,490

Includes:

Hi-tech training course, internships, housing, Hebrew Ulpan, bus pass, field trips, tech tours, medical insurance, educational & professional seminars, 24/7 staff support and more. Flights, food, and spending money are not included.

- **What are living arrangements like:** Apartments in Downtown Jerusalem and Tel Aviv
- **# of Meals**: not included—students are expected to learn life skills on our program (how to cook, clean, budget, buy groceries, etc.)
- **Trips:** At least once or twice a week

- **Any other activities or accommodations included in cost:** Please contact for more details.
- **Additional add on (that can affect cost):** A choice of one international trip per Semester. First semester—choice of Spain, Czech Republic, China; second semester—choice of Ethiopia, Italy, Germany and Poland)

Religious Observance and/or Program Philosophy:

Inclusive (all welcome and everyone will be able to keep their level of observance)

Program Highlights:

- Hi-tech boot camps where you can learn app development or graphic design.
- Weekly trips: dig into the start-up nation. Network and meeting interesting people from all over the world.
- Internships at innovative start-up companies and making an impact in real people's lives with digital solutions.

Student Highlights:

- Meeting people from all over the world
- Living in Jerusalem and Tel Aviv
- The end of IMPACT month when the mayor comes to see us present our technological solutions to our charities and non-for-profits.

BINA GAP YEAR

gapyear@bina.org.il • https://www.bina.org.il/en/gap/

Description of Program:

The BINA Gap Year Program offers the opportunity to make a difference with diverse populations in need in South Tel Aviv. On both our Mechina an Shnat Sherut programs, you will take part in critical and interactive learning about Israeli society, Jewish history, and modern Israel. You will gain leadership skills through planning events for your group or trips across Israel. You'll do all of this with Israeli peers as the programs are fully immersive experiences as you live, learn, and volunteer alongside Israelis your own age.

Length of Program:

10 months

Location of Program:

Tel Aviv

Supervision:

Each group has an English-speaking program counselor (madrich/a)

Cost Range:

$17,500. Full room & board, food, transportation in Tel Aviv, classes, activities, and trips. Additional perks include:

- Volunteer coordination & supervision
- Guidance, mentorship, support
- Amazing community and friends

  - **What are living arrangements like:** Shared apartments
  - **# of Meals:** One to two meals provided each day

- **Trips:** North, south, Jerusalem, borders
- **Any other activities or accommodations included in cost:** Please contact for more details
- **Additional add on (that can affect cost):** Courses available for college credit at additional cost

Religious Observance and/or Program Philosophy

Secular/Pluralistic

Program Highlights:

- Hebrew immersion and integration with Israelis
- Focus on social justice and "tikkun olam"
- Full year in Israel's modern and diverse city of Tel Aviv

Student Highlights:

"I've spent my days learning at BINA's South Tel Aviv based secular yeshiva, applying ancient Jewish texts to our understanding of contemporary Israel. The Gap Year program attracts international students and Israelis alike, all interested in creating a rich relationship with Judaism outside of its traditional religious expressions."

—Ariela

"There truly is no other Gap program like BINA. The combination of social justice and action, learning at the secular yeshiva, living and learning with Israelis, and so much more is so incredibly special, and I feel so lucky to have been on this program."

—Meitav

"BINA Gap Year taught me how to live on my own, how to be responsible for myself and for others, to balance a budget, to balance my time, to be independent. It introduced me to different places in Israel, to different political and social opinions, to different kinds of people, to what it means to live in a group, and so much more. I would definitely recommend it."

—Elya

FRONTIER ISRAEL

https://www.amhsi.org/programs/frontier-israel
Marni Heller • mheller@jnf.org

Description of Program:

The Alexander Muss Institute for Israel Education (AMIIE-JNF) is excited to announce the launch of its inaugural gap semester program: Frontier Israel. Designed by the expert educators at the Alexander Muss Institute for Israel Education (AMHSI-JNF), this program will provide a real life, modern day pioneering experience for incoming freshmen and rising sophomores attending US academic institutions. Frontier Israel will be comprised of two components: meaningful volunteer work in three enriching regions of Israel (Negev, Galilee, and Center) and educational explorations designed to broaden horizons and build a student's portfolio of experiences.

Length of Program:

September to December

Location of Program:

Ben Gurion University, Hod Hasharon, and Moshav Ben Ami

Supervision:

The group will have an educator and two madrichim (counselors).

Cost Range:

$15,000

- **What are living arrangements like:** Lodging, meals, medical insurance, transportation around Israel, and laundry included.
- **# of Meals:** Please contact for more details
- **Trips:** Weekly

- **Any other activities or accommodations included in cost**: Please contact for more details
- **Additional add on (that can affect cost)**: Please contact for more details

Religious Observance and/or Program Philosophy:

Pluralistic

Program Highlights:

- Meaningful volunteer work in three enriching regions of Israel (Negev, Galilee, and Center).
- Volunteer opportunities include farming, building hiking paths for the disabled, working with refugees, and more.
- Educational explorations designed to broaden horizons and build a student's portfolio of experiences. Seminars will include learning retreats to enable students to explore Israel in greater depth through hiking, educational trips, and guest lectures.

GAP YEAR PROGRAM AT BEN-GURION UNIVERSITY OF THE NEGEV

https://in.bgu.ac.il/en/international/Pages/Gap-Year-Program.aspx
https://in.bgu.ac.il/en/international/Pages/default.aspx
Ben Blechman: Recruitment Coordinator, BGU International
bblechman@aabgu.org

Description of Program:

BGU offers young adults the opportunity to spend their Gap Year in a fruitful academic experience while having a meaningful social adventure. As a Gap Year student, you will be part of the study abroad program, enjoying the vibrant campus life, participating in volunteering projects, and studying alongside undergraduate students. As BGU is academically recognized worldwide, the academic credits you will accumulate during the semester at BGU can be accepted as credits toward a future degree at other universities. The varied range of undergraduate courses offered at BGU can help you find your future path. The program is co-ed but men and women are separated in their living accommodations.

Length of Program:

Participants can stay for a semester to a full school year.

Location of Program:

Ben-Gurion University of the Negev in Beer Sheva, Israel

Supervision:

We have professional staff in the BGU International office on campus that are available to students. In addition, student staff members are in charge of social activities and the dorms.

GAP YEAR PROGRAM AT BEN-GURION UNIVERSITY OF THE NEGEV

(Continued)

Cost Range:

Semester Program Base Tuition: $7,200
Year Program Base Tuition: $11,200

Tuition fees for all semester or year-long programs include weekly social activities, academic field trips, trips around Israel, access to the university sports center, and health insurance.

- **What are living arrangements like:** The dormitories are apartments of four private bedrooms with a bathroom, kitchen and shared common area. Each bedroom has a bed, desk, closet, chair and lamp and can be locked for privacy. The apartments have central air-conditioning system.
  Please Note: Aside from furniture, the dorms are unequipped. This means that students have to bring their own linens, pillows, blankets, kitchenware, cooking equipment, and eating utensils. These can easily be purchased locally at a reasonable price and often the Israeli roommates have already bought many of these items.
- **# of Meals:** Please contact for more details.
- **Any other activities or accommodations included in cost:** Academic field trips and trips around Israel are included in the cost of the program. Past trips have included visiting Tel Aviv, Jerusalem, hikes in the Negev Desert, and hikes in Northern Israel.
- **Additional add on (that can affect cost):**
  Fall semester program on campus housing: $2,250
  Spring semester program on campus housing: $2,900

GAP YEAR PROGRAM AT BEN-GURION UNIVERSITY OF THE NEGEV

(Continued)

Year program on campus housing: $4,900
Ulpan for both semester and year programs: $1,500

Religious Observance and/or Program Philosophy:

Although the program itself is not associated with any particular branch of Judaism, we are very supportive of individual choice. For those interested, Hillel, Moishe House, and synagogues are available to students should they choose to attend.

Program Highlights:

- Participants will take classes and potentially live with Israeli students. They will also be integrated with international students from all of the world.
- Merge into BGU's social life—join student union's festivities and events and experience the unique BGU social life. In addition, BGU has been involved in community action and is committed to social change, with the understanding that research and education go hand in hand. Our faculty members and students take part in programs for social initiatives that seek to empower disadvantaged populations while enriching the lives of all involved.
- Students wills have the opportunity to participate in the summer pre-semester intensive Hebrew language course (Ulpan), which is a chance for participants to get to acclimate to Beer Sheva and the BGU Campus earlier. It is also a chance for students to meet other participants earlier.

70

GAP YEAR PROGRAM AT BEN-GURION UNIVERSITY OF THE NEGEV

(Continued)

Student Highlights:

"Not only did this program offer a terrific academic experience, but there was an incredible effort from the staff to immerse you into the culture."
      —Heather

"The faculty of the BGU International are great, very friendly and welcoming, and always willing to help. A fantastic choice for people coming from all parts of the globe who want to experience Israel uniquely. Choosing to go to Israel was the best choice I made and choosing the Overseas Student Program enhanced my experience."
      —Alessa

"The counselors and other support staff were always available and very helpful."
      —Ronnette

GARIN TZABAR

https://garintzabar.org
Amir Lavi • amir@zofim.org.il • +972.2.621.6497

Description of Program:

Garin Tzabar creates a group framework of guidance and support for young Jews and Israelis living abroad who choose to return to Israel or make Aliyah for the first time in order to serve a full and meaningful service in the IDF. This is done by a mental and emotional preparation process that starts in the countries of origin and continues with their arrival to Israel and absorption into the kibbutzim Israeli society and through the processes of military recruitment. The core of the program is carried out during their military service where they continue to live as a group and receive from the group constant guidance and support.

Length of Program:

5 months

Location of Program:

Please contact for more details

Supervision:

Please contact for more details

Cost Range:

$11,000, includes housing and meals

- **What are living arrangements like:** Dorm style accommodation, but you will have a host family in the community for Friday dinners etc.
- **# of Meals:** Please contact for more details

- **Trips:** Please contact for more details
- **Any other activities or accommodations included in cost:** Please contact for more details
- **Additional add on (that can affect cost):** Please contact for more details

Religious Observance and/or Program Philosophy:

Pluralistic

Program Highlights:

- The preparation process: Acceptance to the Garin Tzabar program involves participation in several significant preparation and screening seminars held in parallel at several sites.
- The absorption process: The absorption period includes the period from the opening ceremony on the day of commencement of the program through to the last day of recruitment to the IDF in that cycle.
- Service in the IDF: Upon recruitment in the IDF, the Garin Tzabar program continues to be a warm and supportive home for the Garin members, who continue to enjoy the benefits of the program along with personal guidance and support in solving problems.

HABONIM DROR WORKSHOP

www.hdnaisrael.org/workshop
www.facebook.com/hdnaworkshop
programs@habonimdror.org • 215-595-8092

Description of Program:

Workshop, the longest running program of its kind, is all about giving participants the tools they need to work for social change in Israel. Participants will have the opportunity to volunteer in agriculture on a kibbutz and work in youth education with Jewish and Arab-Israeli youth from Habonim Dror's Israeli sister youth movement, HaNoar HaOved v'HaLomed. Along the way, participants will go through Workshop's one-of-a-kind curriculum on Judaism, Hebrew, and *hadracha* (leadership), and learn about Israeli society through a mix of day innovative courses and day trips. The first two months of the program takes place on Kibbutz Ravid. After those two months, participants will move together to Haifa.

Length of Program:

4 month option: September to December
6 month option: September to March

Location of Program:

Kibbutz Ravid, Haifa

Supervision:

There are anywhere between two to three madrichim (counselors) for the Workshop program. These madrichim do not live with the participants. During the second part of the program, the participants are living in a house/apartment of their own and live independently together.

Cost Range:

4 months: $10,900
6 months: $13,100

The Workshop program tuition includes all educational programming, seminars and day trips, food, housing, living expenses, ground transportation within Israel, and health insurance. Program tuition does not include airfare to and from Israel, so each participant is responsible for finding their own flights to Israel.

- **What are living arrangements like:** Participants will live in shared rooms, each of which is equipped with a bathroom, during their time on Kibbutz Ravid. This is part of the Ravid seminar center. While in Haifa, participants live in an apartment together.
- **# of Meals:** Participants will receive a weekly stipend as part of the program tuition to buy their own groceries and make their own meals. On Kibbutz, they will have some meals provided for them.
- **Trips:** At least once a week during the Kibbutz stay, participants will travel outside of the Kibbutz to participate in educational day tours. These tours complement that week's educational module. There are also seminars on the weekends that will take participants to sites within Israel.
- **Any other activities or accommodations included in cost:** The Workshop program tuition does not cover a special fund called kupa, which is a communal fund set up by participants themselves to cover expenses not covered by the program, such as personal travel and entertainment. Kupa is a fundamental part of the Habonim Dror ideology—it teaches the art of living together based on a system of "give what you can, take what you need." The

workshop group will set up a bank account which will hold their kupa fund, and they will have autonomy to decide how they want to manage that money. The suggested sliding scale for kupa is $600 to $1100.

- **Additional add on (that can affect cost):** Please contact for more details.

Religious Observance and/or Program Philosophy:

Habonim Dror Workshop is a pluralist program. Most participants would identify themselves as secular and non-traditionally observant. We leave it to each participant and to the group of participants on the program to decide how they wish to observe the laws of Kashrut together.

Program Highlights:

- Habonim Dror works in connection with the largest youth movement in Israel, HaNoar HaOved VeHalomed. Our participants will volunteer with youth in HaNoar HaOved VeHalomed's youth centers and clubs. Because of our partnership with HaNoar HaOved, a movement with over 100,000 chanichim from every sector of Israeli society, Workshop participants are tapped into Israeli society, working with a diverse populations such as rich and poor, Jewish and Arab, centre and periphery, and more.
- A unique aspect of the Habonim Dror Workshop program is the emphasis placed on the group experience. Participants are placed in small cohorts, or kvutzot, with whom they share their day-to-day living with as well as many personal experiences. Living communally means that participants learn to take responsibility over themself as individuals as well as others. Participants will make

decisions together, take responsibility for their own schedules, living spaces, and the general flow of their lives on the program.

- Participants on Workshop work in agriculture on Kibbutz Ravid. Agriculture is one of the most important ways for participants to understand and connect themselves to the people and the land of Israel, learn skills in the field of agriculture, and to be active, contributing members of the kibbutz community and to Israeli society.

HEVRUTA GAP YEAR PROGRAM – SHALOM HARTMAN INSTITUTE

https://www.hartman.org.il/program/
hevruta-gap-year-program/
office.hevruta@shi.org.il • +972-2-5675390 • +927-54-4274534

Description of Program:

Hevruta invites Israelis and North Americans to establish a joint pluralistic community founded on discourse and values in the heart of Jerusalem. The program is open to young men and women from all over Israel and North America, from religious and secular backgrounds, who represent a variety of worldviews. Hevruta's goal is to demonstrate how a diverse community that celebrates learning and social engagement can promote tolerant dialogue in the Jewish world by generating a positive identity discourse based on shared aims and beliefs.

Hevruta operates according to three guiding principles – learning, social engagement, and community life. Graduates of the program acquire skills that support leadership, meaningful discourse, and social engagement, which will go on to serve them as they address some of the most significant challenges facing the Jewish People today.

Length of Program:

9 months

Location of Program:

Jerusalem

HEVRUTA GAP YEAR PROGRAM - SHALOM HARTMAN INSTITUTE

(Continued)

Supervision:

Four program counselors live with and guide the participants throughout the year.

Cost Range:

All program costs are included in the tuition aside from air fare and personal spending money. Please contact for program cost details.

- **What are living arrangements like:** Apartment building. Up to three participants in a room and up to eight same-sex participants in an apartment.
- **# of Meals:** Three meals a day, two are cooked by the participants in the apartments and one is catered. Shabbat meals are fully catered.
- **Trips:** Five trips and five one-day tours across Israel throughout the year, all of which are included in the tuition.
- **Any other activities or accommodations included in cost:** Health insurance, culture events, special holiday activities, special dietary needs (to a limit), public transportation in Jerusalem (for program needs).
- **Additional add on (that can affect cost):** Any activities during free weekends/nights.

Religious Observance and/or Program Philosophy:

Hevruta is a pluralistic program which promotes multivocality and therefore accepts participants of all religious and non-religious backgrounds, views and practices. The program is Shomer-Shabbat friendly (Shabbat is observed in all the shared spaces and celebrated by the program) and is fully kosher.

Program Highlights:

- Fully integrates Israeli and North American participants.
- Pluralistic Program promoting respectful dialogue in the Jewish world.
- Intellectual program highlighting Jewish thought and taught by world renowned Shalom Hartman Institute scholars.

Student Highlights:

"Hevruta gave me the opportunity to learn both about myself and about my relationship with Israel. I knew I supported Israel but never understood why it was specifically important to me. Hevruta gave me a deeper understanding of Israeli politics and the issues in the region."

—Sara

"Hevruta was the perfect fit for me: A Pluralistic program with Americans and Israelis from a variety of backgrounds meant that I felt totally comfortable both Jewishly and socially. I loved the intellectual conversations both in and out of the classroom, and the deep and meaningful conversations we had as this close group of friends became my family. Spending nine months in this environment shaped me in so many ways, but I'm most grateful for the connections I still have today from Hevruta."

—Galit

HEVRUTA GAP YEAR PROGRAM – SHALOM HARTMAN INSTITUTE

(Continued)

"I went on Hevruta and it opened my eyes to an Israel I never knew. I lived with thirty Israelis and thirty Americans for the year from different Jewish backgrounds in Jerusalem. I studied politics, philosophy, diaspora relations, the conflict, and pluralistic Judaism for what all felt like the first time. I spent shabbats traveling all over Israel to different homes observing shabbat in different ways. I learned that I could be critical about Israel and embrace it with all its flaws. I discovered different ways of celebrating Judaism that finally felt authentic. I grew to be the happiest, most positive version of myself"

  —Dina Kirshner

ISRAEL LACROSSE

https://lacrosse.co.il/program-overview/
David Lasday • david@lacrosse.co.il

Description of Program:

The Israel Lacrosse Association (ILA) aims to promote lacrosse in the Jewish State by allocating resources, programming, and inspiring participation from all over the country. The organization's vision is based on the belief that lacrosse has an important and significant role in strengthening the ties of Diaspora Jewry to Israel.

Length of Program:

Please contact for more details.

Location of Program:

Ashkelon

Supervision:

Please contact for more details.

Cost Range:

- **What are living arrangements like:** Please contact for more details.
- **# of Meals:** Please contact for more details.
- **Trips:** Please contact for more details.
- **Any other activities or accommodations included in cost:** Please contact for more details.
- **Additional add on (that can affect cost):** Please contact for more details.

Religious Observance and/or Program Philosophy

Please contact for more details.

Program Highlights:

- *Academics*: While Israel Lacrosse provides significant internship opportunities, as well as basic classes in Hebrew, coaching, etc., and broad options for extra-curricular programming, our participants are encouraged to enroll in online classes to study throughout their Israel Lacrosse experience. While our days will be filled and online education is not required, virtual classes offered by US-based institutions are becoming increasingly popular and one to two classes per semester an excellent complement to our regular offerings.
- *Train with the best:* Gap-year participants will prepare on an NCAA regiment with daily lacrosse practice and bi-weekly strength/conditioning sessions. All athletes will be guided through training, preparation for competition, and general mentorship by our world class coaches and specialists.
- *Gap-year participants will participate in Israel Lacrosse's formal coach certification program* before taking the reigns as youth coaches for teams in Ashkelon and the surrounding communities, forging direct relationships with young athletes and their families. Players will build communication skills and serve as direct mentors for youth and leaders in their communities. Our gap-year participants will also serve as general ambassadors throughout the year, making regular "brainstorming" visits to local schools, taking over phys-ed classes to promote the sport and recruit new players, as well as staffing local events and festivals where Israel Lacrosse has a presence.

ISRAEL XP AT BAR ILAN UNIVERSITY

israelxp.com • info@israelxp.com

Description of Program:

Are you looking for a multi-faceted experience that combines university learning with Jewish growth, seeing the land of Israel, and connecting with amazing role models? Then Israel XP at Bar Ilan University is the perfect program for you! Israel XP at Bar Ilan University is a unique Gap Year program. Spend the year after high school in Israel strengthening your Jewish identity. At Israel XP, you will experience:

- Stimulating university courses.
- Inspirational Jewish learning and growth at your own pace.
- Amazing trips across the Land of Israel.
- Uplifting Shabbatons in breathtaking locations.
- And a vibrant group of unforgettable rabbis, teachers and friends.

Length of Program:

September/October to May/June

Location of Program:

Ramat Gan, Israel

Cost Range:

$24,500; tuition includes all classes and credits; trips; dormitory; volunteer options; night activities

- **What are living arrangements like:** Dormitory
- **# of Meals:** Our optional meal plan is kosher and customizable. Please contact for more details
- **Trips:** Please contact for more details

- **Any other activities or accommodations included in cost:** Please contact for more details
- **Additional add on (that can affect cost):** Please contact for more details

Religious Observance and/or Program Philosophy:

Modern Orthodox

Program Highlights:

- The Israel XP student dorms are located in Ramat Ef'al, in the heart of central Israel. Ramat Ef'al lies between Ramat Gan and Kiryat Ono, adjacent to Tel HaShomer hospital, and a brief walk to the Aluf Sadeh bus stop.
- Bar Ilan University is located less than ten minutes away, in Givat Shmuel. On Mondays through Thursdays, private buses shuttle students back and forth to the Bar Ilan University campus.
- The dorms are just a fifteen-minute cab ride from downtown Tel Aviv, and an hour from Jerusalem, with nearby bus stops to both.

KIBBUTZ ULPAN PROGRAM AND CLASSIC VOLUNTEERING PROGRAM

Kibbutz Program Center, 25 Broadway 9th Floor, New York NY 10004
www.kibbutzprogramcetner.net • mail@kibbutzprogramcenter.org
Miki Golod • mail@kibbutzprogramcenter.org • (212) 462 2764

Description of Program:

Kibbutz Ulpan:
This is a MASA recognized program. The Ulpan program takes place in seven different kibbutzim in Israel, twice a year in each one. Participants study Hebrew with teachers certified by the Israeli Educational Ministry and also do some volunteer work on the kibbutz. Participants get to experience kibbutz life, celebrate holidays with the community, travel around the country, meet new people their age from around the world and learn about the different aspects of kibbutz life.

Classic Volunteering:
Volunteers get to choose when they want to start and finish. There's a minimum of two months and maximum of one year. Volunteers get room and board, three meals a day, and health insurance. They enjoy free access to most of the kibbutz facilities. In exchange, they work for the kibbutz during the day, each kibbutz has different work opportunities but expect to mainly work outside. The program is very affordable compared to others. There are no Hebrew classes or extra trips or activities as part of this program.

Length of Program:

Ulpan: 5 months
Classic Volunteering: 2 months to 1 year

KIBBUTZ ULPAN PROGRAM AND CLASSIC VOLUNTEERING PROGRAM

(Continued)

Location of Program:

Ulpan:
Ma'agan Michael, Yagur, Sde-Eliyahu, Mishmar He'Emek, Ein Ha'Shofet, Na'an, Tzuba

Classic Volunteering:
One of many kibbutzim in the list.

Supervision:

There's an assigned person in each kibbutz in charge of the Ulpan group or Volunteers group. However, participants are treated as adults and are expected to be mature, responsible, and reliable.

Cost Range:

Ulpan:
Program cost is $6,300 before the Masa grant. Participants pay the difference between the full price and their Masa grant. Cost includes room and board, meals, trips, classes, health insurance.

Classic Volunteering:
Cost is $840, includes room and board, meals, health insurance.
Flight cost and transportation not included.

- **What are living arrangements like:** Please contact for more details
- **# of Meals:** Please contact for more details
- **Trips:** Please contact for more details

KIBBUTZ ULPAN PROGRAM AND CLASSIC VOLUNTEERING PROGRAM

(Continued)

- **Any other activities or accommodations included in cost:** Please contact for more details
- **Additional add on (that can affect cost):** Please contact for more details

Religious Observance and/or Program Philosophy

Both Kibbutz Ulpan and Classic Volunteering welcome everyone and provide a safe and inclusive environment. We are not affiliated with any specific philosophy but in general kibbutzim are secular. Participants get Shabbat off and are free to observe it. Kibbutz Sde Eliyahu specifically is a Modern Orthodox kibbutz, Shabbat is observed and food is kosher.

Program Highlights

- Experience kibbutz life
- Learn how to speak Hebrew like an Israeli
- Travel around the country and meet new friends

KIVUNIM

www.kivunim.org
info@kivunim.org • 917-658-5884

Description of Program:

KIVUNIM succeeds in delivering an immersive and transformative Gap Year experience of serious academic study, focused international travel and cross-cultural dialogue. These take place within the context of impressive intellectual and aesthetic exploration and growth that develops and deepens our students' Jewish identity as engaged global citizens. All genders and gender nonconforming students accepted.

KIVUNIM students forge a lifelong connection with Israel and the Jewish people through intentionally-designed travel experiences that impart what other Jewish education programs can only envy: a nuanced and integrated understanding of Jewish civilization through sophisticated contact with the remarkable spectrum of religious traditions, cultures, and worldviews among which the Jewish people grew throughout our 2,000-year Diaspora. Students take four core classes—Hebrew, Arabic, Land, People, Ideas: The Challenge of Zionism, and Civilization and Society: Homelands in Exile. They also have the opportunity to volunteer at an organization on a weekly basis. Students live in Jerusalem at Beit Shmuel, and travel to about ten other countries throughout the course of the year.

Length of Program:

January to July 2021, with a possible option of starting in October for immersive Hebrew and Arabic courses.

Location of Program:

Homebase is Beit Shmuel in Jerusalem. Students also travel to Greece, Bulgaria, India, Morocco, Spain, Portugal, Czech Republic, Germany, Italy.

KIVUNIM

(Continued)

Supervision:

We have two to three Resident Advisors that live and travel with the students. We also have a Gap-Year Director who is at the base daily and travels on all international trips. We have other senior staff and language teachers that are at the base during the week and will travel to the international countries as well.

Cost Range:

$55,125. This includes a roundtrip flight from the US, all international travel expenses, room and board, application fee and tuition.

- **What are living arrangements like:** Dorm style living. two to four students per room with private bathroom. Dining hall, classrooms, outdoor and indoor common spaces are located at the base. Students can also have access to the gym at the YMCA around the corner.
- **# of Meals:** Please contact for more details
- **Trips:** Please contact for more details
- **Any other activities or accommodations included in cost:** Please contact for more details
- **Additional add on (that can affect cost):** In order to receive an official transcript from Hebrew College, students are required to pay an additional $1,500.

Religious Observance and/or Program Philosophy:

We accept students with a wide range of religious backgrounds and observances, and do not adhere to one form of observance. We are a kosher program in Israel and when we travel. When traveling, we will only serve vegetarian food if kosher is not an option, and will bring kosher food if necessary.

Program Highlights:

- We are accredited through the Hebrew College and students can receive up to thirty college credits. KIVUNIM students have transferred these credits to a wide variety of North American colleges (e.g., University of Michigan, Emory University, University of Maryland, Washington University in St. Louis, University of Illinois, SUNY Binghamton, Colby College, Ithaca College, Columbia University, University of California at Berkeley, McGill University, etc.).

- Volunteer service work in one of the many meaningful projects that serve the social needs of the Jerusalem community is a key element of our program, devoting as we do one full day each week to "Social Responsibility" placements. As KIVUNIM students are guests in Jerusalem for the year, we feel it is vitally important to give back to "our host." We have developed relationships with many meaningful projects all allowing our students to feel that they are contributing directly to improving the social fabric of Jerusalem.

- In addition to the formal academic program, there are supplemental sessions in music, dance, cuisine, literature, art, and film related to both Israel and the countries of our travels. One night each week is devoted to yet other study opportunities, sponsored either by KIVUNIM or other institutions in Jerusalem. Some study Talmud, others Basic Judaism, some with KIVUNIM staff and others at other Jerusalem Institutions. The KIVUNIM environment is constantly alive with new ideas and discoveries.

Student Highlights:

"I can more clearly see how KIVUNIM truly helped change my perspective and made me more deeply appreciate the important things in life. A lot of my work now involves tackling problems to help those around the world without access to proper healthcare, especially those from different cultures than my own . . . I don't believe I would have been inspired to take on these challenges if not for KIVUNIM having planted the seed of building world consciousness ten years ago."

—MDJ

"Even a decade later, I still consider my gap-year on KIVUNIM one of the most formative experiences of my life. KIVUNIM offered me the opportunity to explore Judaism, Zionism, and globalization through deep, transformative, and personal engagement with these issues. But more than anything, KIVUNIM shaped my identity and enhanced my personal development; because of KIVUNIM, I consider myself a braver, more curious, and more confident citizen of the world."

—ZJ

"I had the most beautiful, inspiring year of my life on KIVUNIM. It made me feel powerful and at home in the world, and I know that I will take my experiences with me throughout life. When I got home, my friends noticed I had become more mature and thoughtful, and I feel that way too. It was truly a blessing to be part of this journey, and I'm so thankful for the opportunity."

—Student

KOL AMI

https://www.kolami.org.il
Naomi Lichenstein • naomi.kolami@gmail.com

Description of Program:

Kol Ami was founded out of a deep understanding that the most effective way to build a sustainable connection between Jewish youth and the State of Israel is by creating personal relationships with the people of Israel. We also believe that the best way to create meaningful personal relationships is by spending time together—Israelis, and Jewish peers from across the globe. Kol Ami was founded in order to address this issue and create a Gap Year program that will connect Israelis and Jewish peers from across the globe.

Length of Program:

6 to 10 months

Location of Program:

Please contact for more details

Supervision:

Please contact for more details

Cost Range:

$11,000, before Masa Israel scholarship and grant; includes room, board, tuition and activities during program time. Additional scholarships & grants may be available. Please contact us for more details.

- **What are living arrangements like:** Participants will be in rooms of between three to five with en-suite bathroom and toilets.
- **# of Meals:** Please contact for more details

- **Trips:** Please contact for more details
- **Any other activities or accommodations included in cost:** Please contact for more details
- **Additional add on (that can affect cost):** Please contact for more details

Religious Observance and/or Program Philosophy:

Secular. Everyone welcome.

Program Highlights:

- *Jewish identity*: Jewish education that emphasizes the uniqueness of the different Jewish communities and ideologies across the globe as well as the common thread connecting all Jewish people. Our Jewish studies programs include classic Jewish studies and contemporary Jewish philosophy, Jewish text, and modern writings.
- *Love for Israel:* High-level Israel education that includes both in-class studies and outdoor activities such as trips/hikes across the country with the goal to connect with the people, the history, the land, and the culture.
- Most importantly, *all the classes are based on discussions and peer-learning.* With participants from twenty-three countries and hundreds of Jewish communities from abroad and Israel, the discussions are fascinating. Women and men from all the streams of Judaism—we make sure that all voices and opinions are heard. Together we create a beautiful community of the next generation of Jewish leaders. Definitely not uniformed, but certainly unified!

MASA YEAR OF SERVICE WITH AARDVARK ISRAEL AND IVA

https://aardvarkisrael.com/masa/ • info@aardvarkisrael.com
USA: 646-844-7784 • Whatsapp: +972-52-429-3681

Description of Program:

Aardvark Israel and the Israel Volunteer Association (IVA) have combined to give Diaspora Jewish youth the opportunity to do "Sherut Leumit"—a year of National Service in Israel.

Sherut Leumi is a program of social service, which gives young people the opportunity to work voluntarily in the sectors of society that need it the most. The participants will be able to choose their volunteering program within the areas of health, education, welfare, and co-existence. Students will volunteer four days a week in the place of their choice and then one day a week will be dedicated to experiential Israel and Jewish education. That day, students will engage in field trips, educational seminars, Hebrew Ulpan, and other enrichment activities. Students will work side-by-side with Israelis, getting a full immersion experience and learn to become independent by living in apartments in the middle of Haifa.

Length of Program:

10 months

Location of Program:

Haifa

MASA YEAR OF SERVICE WITH AARDVARK ISRAEL AND IVA

(Continued)

Supervision:

There is one madrich to twenty students plus a program coordinator and supporting senior staff

Cost Range:

$13,500 to $15,000, with local housing, health insurance, educational trips and seminars, volunteering, local transportation pass, monthly food stipend, staffing and activities

- **What are living arrangements like:** Apartments
- **# of Meals:** Students get a monthly stipend but are expected to buy their own food and cook in the apartments–a goal of the program is for students to learn life skills on the program
- **Trips:** Throughout the program we will have various trips, some locally and some around Israel to show students some of Israel's most special and unique places
- **Any other activities or accommodations included in the cost:** Please contact for more details
- **Additional add on (that can affect cost):** Flight and spending money

Religious Observance and/or Program Philosophy:

Inclusive (everyone welcome—people will be able to keep whatever level of religious observance they like)

MASA YEAR OF SERVICE WITH AARDVARK ISRAEL AND IVA

(Continued)

Program Highlights

- Four weekly days of volunteering (thirty-two hours) in health, education or welfare
- Educational seminar days all over the country. Weekly Hebrew study.
- Pedagogical support and guidance that fosters personal development. Workshops on different topics and holiday activities.

NATIV COLLEGE LEADERSHIP PROGRAM IN ISRAEL

www.nativ.org
Nativ@uscj.org • 646-519-9246

Description of Program:

Nativ is a challenging academic and volunteer year program that aims to create and inspire the Conservative Jewish leaders of tomorrow. The program has two main components: the first semester is an academic semester in Jerusalem where the students have a full load of courses at Hebrew University, or The Conservative Yeshiva, or Ulpan Milah. The second semester is focused on volunteering in small communities around Israel, with the central goals being giving back to others and getting to know Israeli society from within. Throughout the year, Nativ offers a series of seminars about Conservative Judaism, Israel activism, and leadership, all of which are in preparation to return to the North American campuses and Jewish communities.

Yozma is a new inclusion track on Nativ and is dedicated to furthering the development of life and leadership skills that are essential for young adults with cognitive and social challenges to lead independent, meaningful Jewish lives and successfully transition to a college program. These students are fully integrated into the program but are provided with additional support in order to be successful.

Length of Program:

9 months

NATIV COLLEGE LEADERSHIP PROGRAM IN ISRAEL

(Continued)

Location of Program:

Jerusalem for one semester and a small Israeli town for the second semester

Supervision:

Please contact for more details

Cost Range:

Approximately $26,500, including international flight, tuition for academic institution (Hebrew University or other), housing, meals, seminars, hiking trips, health insurance, and all group programs (Yozma track is $41,000, including same as above plus additional staff of ratio two to three partici-pants: one staff member + additional assistant director).

- **What are living arrangements like:** Please contact for more details
- **# of Meals:** Please contact for more details
- **Trips:** Please contact for more details
- **Any other activities or accommodations included in cost:** Please contact for more details
- **Additional add on (that can affect cost):** Spending money for additional food/travel, optional trips to Poland or India during the intersession.

Religious Observance and/or Program Philosophy:

Observant Conservative program—Shabbat observant, fully egalitarian

NATIV COLLEGE LEADERSHIP PROGRAM IN ISRAEL

(Continued)

Program Highlights:

- Studying at Hebrew U (earning up to twenty-one college credits recognized in most US higher academic institutions).
- Full semester of volunteering in a small community, because by being a part of that community forms close relationships with many families/kids, speaking Hebrew.
- Living in a vibrant Conservative community for the entire year—celebrating all of the holidays throughout the year as a community.

Student Highlights:

- "It's a conservative Jewish program and there are very few conservative Gap Year programs in Israel."
- "For the first half of the program you are given the choice to study in a conservative Yeshiva, study Ulpan and improve your Hebrew skills, or study at Hebrew University and get a taste of what college life is like and can earn credit transferring to the university you will be attending post Gap Year."
- "The students live in Jerusalem the first half of the program, and the second half of the program, the students live and volunteer (depending on what they choose) either in Tiberius or Yemin Orde (a youth village—kind of like a kibbutz)."

PIONEER ISRAEL GAP YEAR PROGRAM

https://aardvarkisrael.com/pioneer-israel-gap-year-program/
info@aardvarkisrael.com
• USA: 646-844-7784 • Whatsapp: +972-52-429-3681

Description of Program:

The Aardvark Israel HaShomer HaChadash "Pioneer Israel" Gap Year Program is a fully integrated experience for Israeli and non-Israeli students, and focuses on Jewish values and Zionist identity through strengthening their connections to the land of Israel. As an immersive year of service, participants will forge deep connections to the land and people of Israel while enjoying all the country has to offer. Living in shared apartments, volunteering and learning together, participants will become a tight community, finding common ground as well as celebrating their diversity as they explore the roles and experiences of Jews within and outside of Israel.

The core focus will be the establishment and maintenance of a community garden in Jerusalem. Learning about environmentalism, agriculture, and the geography of Israel, participants will become specialists in these topics to teach Israeli school children and tourists who visit the garden. Hebrew Ulpan, classes about Israel and Judaism, optional twenty-four college credits earned. Field trips, cultural activities, Shabbatonim, and seminars also included.

Length of Program:

10 months (August to May)

Location of Program:

Jerusalem

PIONEER ISRAEL GAP YEAR PROGRAM

(Continued)

Supervision:

One counselor to every sixteen students plus senior supporting staff

Cost Range:

$18,500, with local housing, health insurance, educational trips and seminars, volunteering, local transportation pass, monthly food stipend, staffing, and activities.

- **What are living arrangements like:** Apartments
- **# of Meals:** Students get a monthly stipend but are expected to buy their own food and cook in the apartments—a goal of the program is for students to learn life skills while on the program
- **Trips:** Every other week of the program, students visit the "hidden gems" of Israel
- **Any other activities or accommodations included in cost?:** Evening activities and weekends
- **Additional add on (that can affect cost):** International trips—A choice of one international trip per semester. First semester: choice of: Spain, Czech Republic, China. Second semester: choice of Ethiopia, Italy, Germany, and Poland. Not included are the cost of your flight and spending money.

Religious Observance and/or Program Philosophy:

Inclusive, (everyone welcome—people will be able to keep whatever level of religious observance they like)

PIONEER ISRAEL GAP
YEAR PROGRAM

(Continued)

Program Highlights:

- Living in a Garin, where half the group are eighteen to nineteen-year-old Israelis and the other half are students from the diaspora
- Working the land of Israel, getting to know it and impart your love and knowledge of the land and how to look after it to others
- Being immersed in Israel society and interacting with Israelis all day everyday—amazing for Hebrew immersion

SHNAT NETZER

https://www.shnatnetzer.org.il • wupj@wupj.org.il
Orit Shoshani Sagi • shnat@wupj.org.il • wupj@wupj.org.il
+972-2-620-3447 • 212-452-6530

Description of Program:

Netzer Olami is the global youth movement for engaging youth and young adults in Reform Judaism, operating under the auspices of the WUPJ. We strive to empower and educate youth and young adults with a meaningful Judaism that reflects their beliefs and values, and forms the stepping stones for leading Reform Jewish lives. Shnat Netzer is our global flagship Gap Year program, operating for more than two decades.

Start in Jerusalem, meet change-makers, thought-leaders, activists, and educators working to improve Israeli society and be a part of the Institute for Youth Leaders (Hebrew: Machon Le'Madrichei Chutz La'Aretz). Head to Haifa to experience social, cultural, and political issues first-hand as we meet and volunteer with Israelis working in communal and social action together with young Israelis from Netzer.

Optional add-on: Extension programs so you can dive deeper into those issues that you care most about. Prices for the additional programs vary.

Length of Program:

February to June (check on the specific dates of your year)

Location of Program:

Jerusalem and Haifa

Supervision:

Counselors

SHNAT NETZER

(Continued)

Cost Range:

$10,000, which includes food, commendation, health insurance and travel in Israel. Price does not include flights or spending money during vacations.

- **What are living arrangements like:** Jerusalem: Dorms // Haifa: Apartment
- **# of Meals**: Please contact for more details
- **Trips:** Please contact for more details
- **Any other activities or accommodations included in cost:** Please contact for more details
- **Additional add on (that can affect cost):** Spending money for additional food/travel, optional trips to Poland or India during the intersession.

Throughout the program, you will participate in themed seminars and trips. You will be expected to contribute to the planning and running of these seminars as part of your ongoing leadership (hadracha) training. Seminars serve to deepen your understanding of given topics and many present the opportunity for encounters (mifgashim) with Israelis.

- Jewish identity
- Tiyulim (trips)
- Community seminar
- Israeli-Palestinian conflict & hope seminar
- Tikkun Olam Seminar
- Poland trip

Religious Observance and/or Program Philosophy:

Reform, Progressive

Program Highlights:

- *Discover*: Live in Jerusalem, make new friends from around the world, and travel around Israel to explore historical, political, cultural, and social issues. Meet the change-makers, thought-leaders, activists, and educators working to improve Israeli society and be a part of the Institute for Youth Leaders (Hebrew: Machon Le'Madrichei Chutz La'Aretz), a leading training program of the Jewish Agency for Israel.

- *Action*: Head to Haifa to integrate deeper into Israeli society: experience social, cultural, and political issues first-hand, as we meet and volunteer with Israelis working in communal and social action projects across the city that improve the lives of Israeli Jewish and Arab residents. Practice your Hebrew as you make friends with young Israelis from Noar Telem, the Israeli Progressive youth movement.

- *Featuring:* Optional extension programs, so you can dive deeper into the issues that you care about most, in Israel and around the world. Optional add-ons include: leading on a progressive Jewish summer or winter camp, interning in a WUPJ community, providing humanitarian aid with Project TEN, assisting emergency responders from Magen David Adam, or even building your own Israel experience.

Student Highlights

"Going to Israel with Netzer on Shnat Netzer was the pinnacle of my involvement. It was firstly the best Gap Year one could ever have, in such a complex, exciting, spiritual place. Far better than going to London, like so many South Africans did. It also galvanised the friendships that I have

today, twenty-nine years later. My extensive involvement in the Jewish community and specifically the Progressive Jewish Community may not have happened if I had not gone on Shnat. But the highlight was that it simply was so much fun, I often yearn for that year again!"
—Greg

"The magic of Shnat is that it develops individuals who are well-rounded, competent Jewish youth leaders as well as active and aware human beings. This is done by leading and doing."
—Shira

"Shnat Netzer made me more socially and politically aware, and therefore has given me the confidence to speak out about my opinions both socially and professionally. It's also given me the most understanding and support-ive group of friends around the world. Communal living is also the best uni prep possible as it gives you an understanding of how other people function and how to fend for yourself in a safe environment."
—Sarah

TEL AVIV UNIVERSITY INTERNATIONAL

www.international.tau.ac.il
Jenna Mucciarone: Outreach Coordinator, U.S. Office,
Tel Aviv University International
39 Broadway, Suite 1510, New York, NY 10006
jennam@telavivuniv.org • p: 800.665.9828 ext. 2
f: 212.967.8369
The best way to schedule a phone or zoom meeting with the US
Office is at Jenna's Calendly link: https://calendly.com/jennam-1
For additional information, visit:
https://international.tau.ac.il/Academic_Gap_Year/?id=term-3

Description of Program:

Gap Year or Semester students begin with a mandatory Hebrew Ulpan in order to prepare for life in Israel. Students who are above a Level 8 may be exempt from the Ulpan requirement; please check with your TAU Study Abroad Admissions Coordinator for details (requires a Placement Exam for proof of exemption). You can read more regarding our Hebrew levels and Ulpan program here.

After completing the Ulpan, the academic semester or year begins! Each semester, students take a full schedule of four courses, taught in English from our rich and diverse course schedule. Students can also participate in for-credit Service Learning experiences in order to immerse further into community life here in Tel Aviv and in Israel.

Courses vary from semester to semester, but in general, there is a variety of coursework available in History, Israel Studies, Middle East Studies, Environmental Studies, Jewish Studies, Political Science, Finance, Business, Psychology, International Studies, Arabic, Hebrew, and more!

TEL AVIV UNIVERSITY INTERNATIONAL

(Continued)

Length of Program:

Semester or year

Location of Program:

Tel Aviv, Israel

Supervision:

Our on-campus student life team is comprised of six madrichim who live with the students in the dorms, and our head of student life. The madrichim are available 24/7 to provide ongoing support. This includes orientation on student arrival as well as extracurricular and cultural activities and other things:

- Planning and attending social activities
- Planning and attending excursions
- Providing advice and support on a range of topics
- Assisting with scheduling medical appointments
- Providing immersive opportunities into Israeli life
- Assisting with housing
- Helping with cultural adjustment . . . and much more!

Cost Range:

You can find a full breakdown of costs (including tuition housing and ulpan) on our website. Tuition includes trips, activities, and health insurance.

- **What are living arrangements like:** Housing options include the Einstein dormitories, Broshim dormitories and TAU apartments.

As of Spring Semester 2021, Gap Year/Semester will generally be housed in the new Broshim dormitories.

- **# of Meals:** There is no meal plan, students are responsible for their own meals.
- **Trips:** Two overnight opportunities during each semester, as well as a handful of various local excursions and events.
- **Any other activities or accommodations included in cost:** Please contact for more details
- **Additional add on (that can affect cost):** Please contact for more details

Religious Observance and/or Program Philosophy:

Tel Aviv University is a secular institution which, by virtue of being in the State of Israel, follows a Jewish calendar throughout its academic year. There will be no mandatory academic requirements over Shabbat or any chagim, which means that our international students are able to live as observant a lifestyle as they so choose. We do not have pre-ordained "kosher" apartments, but students are welcome to request either a single occupancy apartment, or housing with students of a similar religious observation.

Program Highlights:

- Earn college credit while gaining life experience in Israel.
- Dedicated student life team of Israeli students to help guide you as you acclimate to a new place.
- Trips and guided tours to help you explore what Israel offers beyond Tel Aviv.

THE HEBREW UNIVERSITY

https://overseas.huji.ac.il/
Michelle Sugarman • msugarman@hebrewu.org

Description of Program:

- Set yourself apart by starting your higher education journey in Jerusalem, a city rich with tradition and full of creativity and innovation.
- Forge connections with Israeli and international students to experience a mosaic of cultures, immersing yourself in Israeli life.
- Benefit from the reputation of the internationally renowned Hebrew University.
- Enjoy full academic support, including meetings with your academic advisor.
- Study at one of the world's top 100 universities.
- Experience diverse activities with new friends.
- Go beyond the classroom and experience Israel through our community service option.
- STEAM program available.

Length of Program:

Semester or year options

Location of Program:

Jerusalem

Supervision:

Academic advisor, student life team

Cost Range:

Semester: $8,100 plus around $2,000 for housing

Full year: $12,700 and around $5,000 for housing

- **What are living arrangements like:** Please contact for more details
- **# of Meals:** Please contact for more details
- **Trips:** Please contact for more details
- **Any other activities or accommodations included in cost:** Please contact for more details
- **Additional add on (that can affect cost):** Please contact for more details

Religious Observance and/or Program Philosophy:

Up to the participant; can request roommate based on Shabbat observance.

Program Highlights:

- Program is based in Jerusalem. A city rich with so much history, culture, innovation, and fun!
- STEAM for social change bridging high-tech and social entrepreneurship program
- Forge connections with international students from over ninety countries while earning college credits and immersing yourself in Israeli life.

Student Highlights:

"My semester abroad at Rothberg was one of the most illuminating, enriching, and best experiences of my life. Many alumni I speak to say the same thing. The Ulpan program was excellent, and the classes were taught by impressive and approachable professors. What I loved most about my semester was meeting other students at Rothberg and the rest of the

university. I was able to connect with many Americans that I've continued to have relationships with here in the U.S., as well as Israelis and
other international students in classes offered by other faculties outside of
Rothberg. Additionally, the types of courses taught in Rothberg allow for
a completely immersive Jerusalem and Israel experience; one day I'd learn
about the City of David, and the next day I'd be physically exploring it! I
am thankful for what Rothberg has given me, and wish other students a
wonderful experience."

—Meitav

"I am a Rothberg alumnus from the spring of 2017! My semester spent
studying abroad at Hebrew University's Rothberg International School was
one of the most enriching and immersive experiences of my life. In addition
to studying Hebrew, Arabic, and general studies courses on the beautiful
campus, I had the opportunity to intern at a local elementary school for
course credit and travel all over the country on weekends. The best parts
of my abroad experience were being able to live independently like a local
in Jerusalem, celebrate some of my favourite Jewish holidays such as Purim
and Yom Ha'atzmaut in a lively atmosphere, making international friends,
and running the Jerusalem marathon.

"The extracurricular activities available to Rothberg students truly enhanced
my experience. I participated in the Thrive at Hebrew U program which provided me with a home away from home, supported me in Jewish learning,
and allowed me to experience the diversity of Israeli society through day
trips and weekend trips. The programming and trips offered by Rothberg's
Office of Student Life were also great resources for adapting to Jerusalem
living and exploring Israeli culture and society. I look back on my Rothberg

experience with immense joy, and am forever thankful to have had such a well-rounded formal and experiential educational opportunity there."

—Joelle

"Studying abroad at Hebrew University was one of the greatest experiences of my life. The people that I met, the classes that I took, and the trips that I went on all pushed me to grow as a person. Meeting people from all over the world with such different backgrounds made me look at everything in a different, more nuanced way. The classes that I took were beyond interesting and topics were offered that I didn't have access to at my home university, such as Kabbalah, Trauma and Resilience, and Experiential Jewish Education. My Hebrew teacher was amazing and helped take my language skills to the next level. The opportunity to go out every day into the real world and engage with Israeli society made all of the difference. I feel so blessed to have had the chance to spend significant time in Israel at that age."

—Jake

WORLD BNEI AKIVA – KIVUN

www.worldbneiakiva.org/kivun
Head of Program: Rabbi Ari Faust • ravari@worldbneiakiva.org

Description of Program:

Based in apartments in Jerusalem, where participants learn to shop, cook, and clean by themselves (with the guidance of our staff)—they then branch out for satellite programs around Israel: Kibbutz, community volunteering, and a choice of MDA or the Marva army course. The program is highlighted by a two-month professional internship, Jewish and Zionist learning, and exceptional tiyulim such as Shvil Yisrael. Throughout the various components of the year, the designated staff guide the group, enhancing their year with shiurim, chavrutot, and special social and education activities that develop their Jewish and Zionist identities. On this program as well, participants will make friends from around the world on other World Bnei Akiva programs.

The program is for independent-minded high school leavers who are highly motivated for a year of growth, engaging with Judaism and experiencing Israel—both in unparalleled fashion. Kivun is a religiously observant program.

Length of Program:

9 months

Location of Program:

Jerusalem/travel

Supervision:

Live-in madrichim

Cost Range:

$26,000, includes accommodation, food, programming, health insurance, travel—all programming related.

- **What are living arrangements like:** Apartments in Jerusalem
- **# of Meals:** Three per day
- **Trips:** Weekly, depending on time of year
- **Any other activities or accommodations included in cost:** Please contact for more details
- **Additional add on (that can affect cost):** Please contact for more details

Religious Observance and/or Program Philosophy:

Modern Orthodox—Religious Zionist, Inclusive. The program guidelines and atmosphere are religiously observant, there can be participants from a range of backgrounds.

Program Highlights:

- Diverse, international group
- Magen David Adom/Marva IDF course choice
- Two-month professional internship

Student Highlights:

"Kivun is like no other experience. Nowhere else will you be fully immersed into Israeli culture and society, and provided with the best tools and opportunities to grow. It gave me a strong sense of identity, opportunities I couldn't imagine, enriching speakers, an inspiring global community, and friends for life. It's an experience of the best Israel has to offer, and will last you a lifetime."

—Sara

"Kivun is like an extended family. It allows you to grow at your own pace whilst challenging you and allowing you to grow in your independence and spiritual beliefs. The program is structurally diverse so that throughout the entire year you have thoroughly learned about the diversity of Israeli culture—from the strenuous life on a kibbutz, what giving your life for the army really means, and how giving without expecting anything in return exceeds all expectations. Kivun is not just a year in Israel, but it's a year when you can say you've learned to walk the life of an Israeli, and to make a tangible difference to Israeli society."

—Shira

"Kivun was a life-changing year. I learned about our heritage, learned how to live independently and learned about myself. I gained invaluable life skills and friends that I'll have my entire life—it was like I got a new family. Kivun was without a doubt, the best year of my life!"

—Benjamin

YACHAD GAP YEAR

http://mechinot.org.il/en-us/yachad
Gal Karmel, Yachad Gap Year Coordinator, Joint Council of
Mechinot yachad@mechinot.org.il • Cell: 972-54-799-2770
What'sApp: +39-327-884-0091

Description of Program:

The Joint Council of Mechinot offers a unique Gap Year program for high school graduates from Jewish communities from around the world. Yachad Gap Year gives you the opportunity to have the ultimate immersion experience in Israel. As a participant, your Israel experience will be more up close and personal than any other—because you will be doing it together with your Israeli peers. Yachad gives you the opportunity for personal development through a combination of studying, hiking, volunteering, experiential learning, and the acquiring of leadership skills. Our framework encourages its participants to develop independent thinking and to enhance their ability to cope with future challenges and the tasks of adult life. Yachad focuses on giving its students the tools to become social leaders whilst exploring and experiencing the Israeli society.

Length of Program:

10 months

Location of Program:

There is a path for everyone! The Mechinot are spread out across Israel in kibbutzim and cities.

Supervision:

Mechina students will be expected to lead different projects and responsibilities in the group, with the guidance of mechina staff members, counselors, and the head of the mechina.

YACHAD GAP YEAR

(Continued)

Cost Range:

$13,650 to $15,000

Mechina tuition includes all educational activities, room, board, mass transit for Mechina activities, health insurance, third-party insurance, and laundry. Participants will stay in the Mechina dorms or apartments.

- **What are living arrangements like:** Please contact for more details
- **# of Meals:** Please contact for more details
- **Trips:** Please contact for more details
- **Any other activities or accommodations included in cost:** Please contact for more details
- **Additional add on (that can affect cost):** Please contact for more details

Religious Observance and/or Program Philosophy:

Yachad offers twelve different Mechinot with different levels of religious observance: Modern Orthodox, Conservative, Reform, Secular, Pluralistic and mixed religious and secular.

Program Highlights:

- Yachad offers abroad students the opportunity to join the Israeli Mechinot and experience Israel from within with the Israeli students (only up to 10% abroad students in each Mechina).
- We believe that in order to get to know Israel, our students should meet its society. One of the focuses of the Mechina is having trips and seminars across Israel, exposing students to a wide variety of views and opinions, which are studied and examined in depth, with respect for freedom of ideas and beliefs.

- Our vision and goals are to help develop strong, valiant leaders who will promote prosperity in Israel or wherever they may choose to be after the Mechina. We believe in modest leadership based on personal example and acceptance toward all mankind.

Student Highlights:

"I'm not sure I've made a better decision than the day I decided I would be coming to the Mechina. Looking back on it, I am so happy that I pushed past my hesitations of language, distance, and culture and embarked on the best journey I've ever taken. The year in the Mechina made me smarter, stronger, more prepared for life, and allowed me to develop a connection to incredible Israeli youth from all over the country, and travel, study, live, volunteer, work and grow with them by my side."

—Matan

"As Walt Disney wisely put it, 'If you can dream it, you can do it.' I used to think that these words were nothing but a fantasy, but in the last ten months, my time at the mechina has taught to see the truth in these nine words. From the daily lectures and the weekly schedules to the trips and the volunteering opportunities, the mechina offers you plenty of room to express who you truly are and/or want to be, you just need to be able to take hold of those opportunities and allow your dreams to become a reality. Looking back, it's amazing to see how many projects I was able to help organize, projects that were once ideas waiting for someone to bring to life."

—Gil

YACHAD GAP YEAR

"At the end of the year I see all that I accomplished, and all the land we cov-ered, and how I endured it all and came out stronge.r, was more meaningful than anything else. I'm thankful to the mechina and the framework of the program for allowing me and giving me the chance to grow and see what I am capable of not only personally, but in a group as well."
 —Lexi

YOUNG JUDAEA'S YEAR COURSE IN ISRAEL (THE ORIGINAL GAP YEAR IN ISRAEL)

www.youngjudaea.org
Pamela Brode, West Coast Recruiter • 747-224-1678

Description of Program:

Young Judaea Year Course in Israel is a nine-month Gap Year program for high school graduates ready to have one incredible year! With semesters in both Tel Aviv and Jerusalem, you'll live in fully furnished apartments or in dormitory-style housing. Explore your passion through interning or volunteering, and take a variety of stimulating courses for college credit. Learn Hebrew intensively and get to know Israel from top to bottom—because the best way to understand Israel's diverse society, history, culture, and geography is to live like an Israeli on your Gap Year in Israel!

You will appreciate Israel as a local rather than as a tourist, and your experiences are fostered by volunteering, learning and speaking Hebrew, traveling around the country, and living with fellow participants from North America, the UK, and Israel. In addition to volunteer placements and academic classes, each Year Course semester is enhanced with a variety of cultural events, seminars, and activities with Israeli peers. Specialty add-on tracks and global trips round out the experience.

Year Course offers the perfect balance of structure and independence, encouraging participants to grow into responsible and worldly leaders at home and abroad! Our alumni are passionate about Israel, Jewish peoplehood, and making a difference in the world.

Length of Program:

9 months

YOUNG JUDAEA'S YEAR COURSE IN ISRAEL (THE ORIGINAL GAP YEAR IN ISRAEL)

(Continued)

Location of Program:

Four months in Jerusalem, four months in Tel Aviv and an adventure month with travel and a variety of experiences throughout Israel. In addition, our students travel to Poland together and additional international trips are available to add on to the program including Morocco, India, Rwanda, and Spain.

Supervision:

Year course maintains a highly qualified administrative and educational staff in Israel under the supervision of its director, Kate Nachman.

Groups are staffed by qualified Israeli, American, and British madrichim (group leaders). Madrichim are selected on the basis of their Jewish and Israeli backgrounds, experience in youth work, as well as emotional stability and maturity. Many of them are Year Course alumni. All American and British counselors are college graduates and all Israeli counselors have completed their required military or national service.

Year Course faculty have extensive experience in formal and/or informal education, have earned, minimally, an M.A. (with the exception of Ulpan teachers) and are approved by the American Jewish University (AJU).

Cost Range:

$26,400

- **What are living arrangements like:** In Jerusalem we on a secure campus at Kiryat Moriah with dorm style living and a dining hall. In Tel Aviv, it is also dorm style living but with kitchens on each floor so our students gain a sense of independence and how to live on their own.
- **# of Meals:** A food stipend is provided in Tel Aviv.
- **Trips:** Included is a trip to Poland and tiyulim and weekly trips throughout Israel.
- **Any other activities or accommodations included in cost:** Medical insurance and most everything our students need in the year is included. They will want to bring some spending money for extra trips they may choose to take with friends on free weekends.
- **Additional add on (that can affect cost):** They can add on to our international trips—India, Rwanda, Portugal, and Morocco.

Religious Observance and/or Program Philosophy:

Young Judaea is a Zionist and Pluralist organization. Our love of the Jewish State of Israel is our main pillar. We are open to all view points and do not push one way of thinking as there are so many perspectives. We seek to share and celebrate them allowing our students to find their own viewpoint.

All of our programs make sure to accommodate all levels of observance. We have students across the religious spectrum from non-affiliated to Modern Orthodox. We keep kosher and celebrate Shabbat, our students do this in all kinds of ways—some are shomer shabbos and others not, but we value and always respect those who do and keep.

YOUNG JUDAEA'S YEAR COURSE IN ISRAEL (THE ORIGINAL GAP YEAR IN ISRAEL)

(Continued)

We are dedicated to the values of *tikkun olam* (world repair), family, and community. By improving participants' literacy in Jewish history and tradition, Hebrew, and contemporary Israeli culture through college-level courses, Year Course fosters a positive sense of Jewish identity preparing participants for a lifetime of Jewish communal engagement.

Program Highlights:

- Young Judaea is the very first Gap Year program in Israel; we have made many contributions to Israeli Society, so much that they named a street after us in Tel Aviv.
- We are a perfect balance of fun, freedom, structure, meaning, and adventure. Our students really experience what Israeli culture is like as we strive to be a part of it and always contribute to society.
- We celebrate our students' individuality and create opportunities for everyone to explore the things they love whether it's through our internships, volunteering on the Magen David Adom (Israeli Ambulance), going on Kibbutz, or our many specialty tracks (business, medical, fitness, coding, and tiyul track).

Student Highlights:

"I knew I wanted to be a part of something bigger than me, bigger than anything I have ever been involved in, something worthy of not just me but others around me. The experiences and friendships I've made have left an everlasting impact on my life and changed me as a person."
    —Adi

YOUNG JUDAEA'S YEAR COURSE IN ISRAEL (THE ORIGINAL GAP YEAR IN ISRAEL)

(Continued)

"Before we arrived, our ideas about Israel were formed through information our friends and family had given us. Seeing Israel through our own eyes allowed us to develop a deeper love and understanding for the culture of the Jewish people."

—Rachel

WOMEN'S PROGRAMS

AMUDIM

https://www.amudimisrael.org • info@amudimisrael.org

Description of Program:

In an innovative beit midrash where students are immersed in both traditional learning and modern scholarship, Amudim provides the intellectually curious student with the necessary toolbox for lifelong independent Torah study. Amudim's staff foster honest conversations about essential and existential issues such as the existence of God, free will, the afterlife, the problem of evil and suffering, the composition of Torah texts, and the interaction between Judaism and modern values and ethics. In addition to our first-rate on-campus faculty, we have regular classes at the Bible Lands Museum, Bar-Ilan campus, the National Library and in the Old City, and weekly seminars featuring internationally renowned experts in their fields. We live our Torah on our tiyulim, whether it's by building Talmudic era stoves to cook for our camping shabbaton or meeting with Ka'arites after hiking in the southern desert. Our internship program allows our students to explore fields that may be of interest professionally for them long term (and help boost their CVs) in fields such as medicine, STEM, academia, archaeology, the arts, animal care, and more.

Length of Program:

10 months

Location of Program:

Modi'in

Supervision:

Our Student Life Coordinator lives on campus, helping the students and madrichot address any issues that arise. Our insurance plan provides twenty-four-hour support, including transportation to and chaperoning during emergency care visits. Amudim students are independent and responsible, trusted to make responsible decisions within the rules cited in our handbook.

Cost Range:

$27,000, with a possibility for scholarships.

- **What are living arrangements like:** Students live in modern, clean, apartments with outdoor spaces, WiFi, functioning kitchens, and laundry rooms.
- **Meals:** Students are provided with 3 meals a day when classes are in session.
- **Trips:** Days of swimming and hiking followed by nights of bonding in the Galil, Golan, and Eilat; Shabbatot spent camping in the great outdoors or in urban Hareidi enclaves, beautiful kibbutzim, Jerusalem and Safed; Day trips shepherding flocks of sheep and harvesting etrogim; These are all essential aspects of the Amudim experience.
- **Any other activities or accommodations included in cost?:** Please contact for more details
- **Additional add on (that can affect cost):** Please contact for more details

Religious Observance and/or Program Philosophy:

Modern Orthodox

AMUDIM

(Continued)

Program Highlights:

- An open minded, intellectually engaged beit midrash where no topic is off limits.
- Special programs and trips with hands on experiences and encounters with unique people that are only done at Amudim.
- Direct access to some of the most renowned orthodox academics through our programs at Hebrew University, Bar Ilan University, and the weekly Amudim Seminar.

Student Highlights:

"We spend our days doing 'frum academia,' exploring literally any topic and ultimately the world with a Jewish lens—through Gemara, Tanakh, philosophy, logic, art, history, literature—and whatever we can pull out of the encyclopedic brains of our teachers. I finally feel like I'm becoming a well-rounded person."

—Zoie

"I love being able to explore Torah and Jewish ideas from multiple perspectives and being given room to think for myself."

—Meira

"The longer I'm at Amudim, the more I realize how much more there is to know. We use both sources and our own minds to draw conclusions. I came to Amudim knowing how to think, but here I'm learning how to think well."

—Avigayil

BAER MIRIAM MAAYANOT

www.baermiriam.com
Rabbi Levi Orbach • ravorbach@gmail.com • 646-402-1646

Description of Program:

Our goal at Baer Miriam is to cultivate in our students a love of learning and to provide the tools for learning; the foundation for a lifelong pursuit of Torah and spiritual growth.

Classes cater to all levels of students, and yet are able to challenge the most advanced. The personal involvement of our teachers, the challenging and inspirational classes, and the "ruach," combine to create an unparalleled learning experience. Baer Miriam aims to integrate Torah into the very fabric of our lives.

There is a tremendous diversity of our classes. We offer various approaches to the study of each subject: textual, contextual, and Hashkafa. In addition to the core curriculum and program requirements, you are able to create your own schedule which best suits your needs and interests.

Length of Program:

September to June

Location of Program:

Har Nof Jerusalem

Supervision:

A lot—dorm mothers, dorm counselors, lots of staff!

Cost Range:

$28,000, entire program

- **What are living arrangements like:** Apartments—beautiful and new (AC and US beds)
- **# of Meals:** Two (low cost meal plan for third—if desired)
- **Trips:** A tremendous amount—shabbatonim tiyulim
- **Any other activities or accommodations included in cost:** Tutoring, volunteering, lots of special activities
- **Additional add on (that can affect cost):** Please contact for more details

Religious Observance and/or Program Philosophy:

Orthodox

Program Highlights:

- Staff
- Trips and accommodations
- Baer Miriam is your family

Student Highlights:

- Our wide variety of teachers and classes create a very comfortable and resourceful environment for girls from all different backgrounds to be able to learn and grow and be focused on individually.
- Our convenient location is in Jerusalem and close to many popular areas, but also not right in the center of the city so it provides a small-town vibe.
- Baer Miriam never closes its dorms—no Shabbos or holiday will you ever be left without a place to go.

DARCHEI BINAH SEMINARY

www.darcheibinah.org
American Office: sf@infodbi.com
Israel Office: info1@darcheibinah.co.il

Description of Program:

Darchei Binah was founded and is directed by noted educators Rabbi & Mrs. Shimon Kurland. Rabbi Nachman Bulman zt"l served as the inspiration behind the creation of the seminary based on his world outlook of the primacy of Torah in all aspects of life. Young Jewish women are encouraged to develop their intellectual and creative abilities to their fullest in the pursuit of this goal.

Length of Program:

September to June

Location of Program:

Ramat Sharett/Bayit Vegan

Supervision:

Eim Bayit visits nightly. Madrichot supervise each dorm. Curfew strictly enforced.

Cost Range:

$24,000

- **What are living arrangements like:** Dormitory
- **# of Meals:** One Shabbat arrangement
- **Trips:** Several overnight tiyulim each year (currently no guarantee due to Covid considerations) as well as whole day and half day tiyulim.

- **Any other activities or accommodations included in cost:** A trip to Poland (currently no guarantee due to Covid)
- **Additional add on (that can affect cost):** Please contact for more details

Religious Observance and/or Program Philosophy:

Orthodox

Program Highlights:

- Emphasis on personal/religious growth and development.
- Strong personal ties forged with staff members.
- Intellectually stimulating classes with world renowned speakers.

MACHON MAAYAN

http://www.machonmaayan.org
Meryl Lee Avraham • office@machonmaayan.org
908-344-5860

Description of Program:

Machon Maayan is a transformative, life-changing seminary journey which combines inspirational, serious Torah learning, diverse and personalized chesed/internship opportunities, and thought-provoking, experiential weekly seminars and tiyulim that seamlessly move the classroom into the Land of Israel. Over the years, Machon Maayan has developed the reputation of being an incredibly warm home where each student is showered with personal attention by a very caring and passionate staff. The multi-facility Givat Washington college campus—which includes an Olympic-size swimming pool, a gymnasium, basketball and tennis courts, a fitness center, an art school, a music school, an Israeli Midrasha, and more—is the perfect address for motivated young women who wish to grow personally, spiritually, and religiously.

Length of Program:

10 months

Location of Program:

The Givat Washington campus

Supervision:

Dorm counselors and house mothers

Cost Range:

$26,000

- **What are living arrangements like:** Modern dorm with three girls to a room, en suite bathroom, and a kitchenette for every four rooms.
- **# of Meals:** Three meals
- **Trips:** Four overnight trips per year
- **Any other activities or accommodations included in cost:** Seminar, where Israel is our classroom every Thursday. Gym, indoor pool, and exercise classes. Monthly shabbatonim on- and off-campus. Rosh Hashana, Yom Kippur, Purim, and Shavout programming. There is an optional shabbaton every shabbat
- **Additional add on (that can affect cost):** Please contact for more details

Religious Observance and/or Program Philosophy:

Religious Zionistic

Program Highlights:

- Seeing and connecting with the Land and people of Israel every week on seminars.
- Emphasis on the individual and building a close family environment.
- Beautiful college campus with lots of amenities and availability to take classes in the other programs on campus such as in the schools of music and art.

Student Highlights:

"Among the many things that make our Gap Year unique, here are three that stand out to me. This program is a once-in-a-lifetime learning experience because there are custom- tailored classes to meet every girl's learning level and interest. Another amazing part of our program is how the learning extends beyond the classroom and bring their learning to life as students are able to see Israel firsthand on the trips that they go on weekly. The campus location is a real added benefit as the rural setting sets the perfect tone for spending a year investing in yourself, spiritually, and socially."

MEOROT YERUSHALAYIM

gomeorot.com
info@gomeorot.com

Description of Program:

Meorot Yerushalayim is the only Gap Year seminary geared exclusively toward students who went to public school or grew up in non-observant homes. Through programs like NCSY, Israel trips and relationships they've built with rabbis and teachers, these young women have been inspired to make Judaism a larger part of their lives. They come to Meorot to find out how.

Every Meorot student is an incredibly motivated group and a warm and inspirational environment.

The curriculum caters to a wide range of educational backgrounds: there are classes for those with no experience with Hebrew or Torah learning and for students who have gained more skills. With twenty to thirty students every year, each young woman can expect individualized attention. Meorot also offers art and medical seminars, chesed opportunities and the chance to explore Israel through trips and Shabbatonim!

Length of Program:

One academic year, September to June

Location of Program:

Jerusalem

Supervision:

Meorot has an exceptionally high staff-to-student ratio. In addition to madrichot and an Eim Bayit (house mother) who lives with the students, Meorot has several teachers and staff members who act as "mentors" to each student. Meorot also has a full-time social worker on staff who ensures that each student is getting what she needs to thrive physically, spiritually, and emotionally.

Cost Range:

Tuition (including room and board) is $24,000—however, many scholarships are available and no student is turned away for financial reasons.

- **What are living arrangements like:** Students live in apartments with comfortable beds (American mattresses)
- **# of Meals:** Three meals a day are provided
- **Trips:** Meorot students go on at least two trips per month, including overnight trips in the North and South of Israel
- **Any other activities or accommodations included in cost:** All trips, Shabbatonim, etc., are included in the cost
- **Additional add on (that can affect cost):** Please contact for more details

Religious Observance and/or Program Philosophy:

Meorot Yerushalayim is an Orthodox program that is designed for students from a variety of backgrounds.

Program Highlights:

- Personalized attention & mentorship throughout the entire year.
- Students who are motivated, inspired, and growth-oriented.
- High-level classes which start from the beginning, to make sure "no steps are skipped" and the students develop a strong foundation.

MEOROT YERUSHALAYIM

(Continued)

Student Highlights:

"My time at Meorot Yerushalayim was truly one of the most life-changing experiences I have ever had. It opened up my eyes and my heart to Torah and Judaism in irreversible ways, and I would do anything to experience it all over again. The memories that I made with the people who have become my best friends will last me a lifetime, and will certainly be passed down many generations. Thanks to Meorot, I was able to begin my journey as a young Jewish woman with a bright future full of Yiddishkeit."
   —Ariel

"At Meorot, I got the chance to attend classes, learn with amazing mentors, travel Israel, and meet some of my best friends. Everyone was so nice, welcoming, and kind from the very start. Whether we were on the bus, in the dorms, at school or on a Shabbaton, the environment was growth- oriented, positive, and fun. I am so grateful to have been able to attend Meorot and I smile every time I look back on memories from my year in seminary."
   —Kayla

"Choosing to go to Meorot was the best decision I ever made. I wanted to go to a place where I could truly take the time to learn about myself, my religion, and my heritage each in depth, building the solid Jewish foundation that I had sought for so long. Not only did Meorot give me this, but it gave me a group of likeminded, lifelong friends and mentors to look up to and continue to guide me beyond my time at Meorot. I learned all that I had hoped for and so much more, and, above all, gained confidence in myself as a Jewish woman that will carry me through my lifetime."
   —Katherine

MICHLALAH

Description of Program:

Michlalah's Machal program strives for excellence in learning and religious commitment, along with a deep appreciation for the land of Israel. Michlalah offers a variety of classes, ranging in style and levels. Michlalah is also located on an Israeli college campus.

Length of Program:

One year

Location of Program:

Bayit Vagan, Jerusalem

Supervision:

Eim Bayit (on-campus resident). Each girl is assigned an advisor and a madricha (counselor). The advisor helps with building a girl's schedule and answering any questions throughout the year. Religious guidance from a variety of mentors.

Cost Range:

Varies, scholarships awarded.

- **What are living arrangements like:** Apartment-style dorms. Groups of twelve, eight, or six girls share a kitchen and bathroom.
- **# of Meals:** One per day (lunch)
- **Trips:** Several throughout the year, including hikes and a week in Eilat.

- **Any other activities or accommodations included in cost:** Access to the campus amenities such as a swimming pool, gym, and library
- **Additional add on (that can affect cost):** Poland heritage trip

Religious Observance and/or Program Philosophy:

Orthodox

Program Highlights:

- Staunch commitment to Halacha (Jewish law).
- Extensive alumni network and legacy.
- Fosters independence, including the academic curriculum each girl builds.

Student Highlights:

- An abundance of courses to choose from, ranging from lecture-style to interactive learning.
- Located on a college campus, thus providing students with access to a variety of facilities.
- Students live in apartments and mini-houses, leading to a living culture that builds group relationships.

MICHLELET MEVASERET YERUSHALAYIM (MMY)

http://www.mevaseret.org/mmy
office@mmy.org.il

Description of Program:

At MMY you will:

LEARN Torah on a very high level.

- We believe that Torah study for women must be conducted seriously, intellectually, and analytically.
- Choices and flexibility allow you to build your perfect schedule.

THINK about issues, relate them to your life and develop your personal philosophy.

- We are deeply committed to the idea that no one form of religious expression is right for everyone.

GROW spiritually as you internalize the beauty and messages of Torah into your life.

- At MMY, we believe that the purpose of all learning must be to inspire & develop genuine religious growth.
- We observe many holidays and special events together as a group.

CONNECT with the Land, People, and State of Israel.

- At MMY, we firmly believe that both Eretz Yisrael (the land of Israel) and Medinat Yisrael (the modern State of Israel) must be central in the life of every Jew.

MICHLELET MEVASERET YERUSHALAYIM (MMY)

(Continued)

Length of Program:

10 months

Location of Program:

Baka, Jerusalem

Supervision:

Seminary with a full supervisory staff

Cost Range:

Approximately $30,000 including room and below details

- **What are living arrangements like:** Please contact for more details
- **# of Meals:** main meal on school days (second meal offered for a small fee)
- **Trips:** All trips; please contact for more details
- **Any other activities or accommodations included in cost?:** Health insurance. Please contact for more details
- **Additional add on (that can affect cost):** Flight not included. Please contact for more details

Religious Observance and/or Program Philosophy:

We are a strongly religious Zionist program

Program Highlights:

- Text-based partner learning program
- Spiritual growth through the intellectual process

MICHLELET MEVASERET YERUSHALAYIM (MMY)

(Continued)

- Warm environment with close connections to teachers and mentors

Student Highlights:

"In MMY I was able to develop the deepest of relationships . . . Each Rabbi/ teacher makes you feel important, validated, and like they truly do care."
—Leora

"MMY was a foundation for my life. MMY helped me solidify my morals, my views, and my goals. It made me who I am—and who I am still becoming."
—Rina

"The partner style learning not only forced us to challenge ourselves, to understand content independently, it also showed us how capable we really are when learning on our own."
—Shoshana

MIDRESHET AMIT

www.midreshetamit.org
midrasha@amit.org.il • 026450435 / US Line: 6464848982

Description of Program:

At Midreshet AMIT, our students spend the day learning, questioning, and growing in Torah. From interesting and challenging classes to guided chavruta study, the year will be packed with learning geared to help develop a lifelong connection to Torah. Our home is in Beit Hayeled, AMIT's well known foster home for disadvantaged youth. Our students will spend time each day teaching, playing, and caring for some of Israel's most needy children. As a "big sister," they are challenged to give of themselves in a way you have never experienced before and are transformed in the process. A connection to Israel will be deepened through the unique experience of living and interacting with dedicated Israeli couples and committed Sheirut Leumi young women. Through adventurous tiyulim, our students will travel the length and breadth of Israel, learning about our history and gaining a greater appreciation for the State of Israel.

Length of Program:

September to June

Location of Program:

Jerusalem

Supervision:

Our dorm is supervised by caring madrichot who serve as role models and are available to assist with making the adjustment as smooth as possible.

MIDRESHET AMIT

(Continued)

Cost Range:

$29,650, includes all classes, trips, three meals a day, and twenty-four-hour security.

- **What are living arrangements like:** Our dorm is made up of suites with comfortable American beds and spacious quality furniture to store your clothing. Each room also has a safe for the girls in the room to use and set with a private code. Each suite is equipped with a full kitchen facility. The common room has a lounge and exercise machines and is equipped with a wireless internet connection for you to use with personal laptops and iPads.
- **# of Meals:** Three
- **Trips:** We have three overnight trips and monthly tiyulim as well. Tanach and Jewish History come to life as we explore the geography of Israel on our tiyulim. Shabbatonim in communities like Gush Etzion, Tsefat, and Beit Shemesh will expose our students to the diverse populations of contemporary Israel. Additionally, we are part of a large network of over 100 AMIT schools throughout the entire country renowned for academic excellence and professionalism. We will visit some of the AMIT schools and participate in joint programs.
- **Any other activities or accommodations included in cost:** Monthly elective courses include unique trips related to themes studied in the classroom.
- **Additional add on (that can affect cost):** Optional Poland Trip

Religious Observance and/or Program Philosophy:

Modern Orthodox, Shomer Shabbat

MIDRESHET AMIT

(Continued)

Program Highlights:

- At Midreshet AMIT, our students have the unique opportunity to engage in meaningful and daily chesed. Our home is Beit Hayeled, AMIT's very special foster home for disadvantaged Israeli children. Our students become part of a "mishpachton," a family unit made up of a caring young Israeli couple and twelve children. Our students have the opportunity to work with the children to provide structure, stability, and love.
- We offer exciting, challenging classes for ALL learners. Toward that end, we have worked hard to ensure that each time slot offers a variety of choices so that students of every level, background, and style can find classes that motivate them to achieve more than they ever thought possible in the world of Talmud Torah.
- Our Beit Midrash time offers daily opportunities to learn one-on-one with a staff member or a friend. Students can accomplish so much and reach the individualized goals they set for themselves.

Student Highlights:

"The Beit Midrash is my unique place at AMIT to find the answers I am searching for. I can choose any topic that I want to learn which takes my personal connection with Judaism to a new level. The Beit Midrash program also allows all of us the ability to build strong relationships with the teachers and our peers through the study of Torah! Observing my friends learning independently or b'chavruta is truly inspiring."

—Raquel

"Volunteering in Beit Hayeled has added a much deeper meaning to my seminary experience. All of the children have such kind hearts and I am lucky that AMIT provides me with the opportunity to support and love them! I spend time in the late afternoons with Claudine who has the most infectious smile. We laugh, play games, and visit animals in the pet therapy area. Our relationship has undoubtedly impacted my life."

—Maya

"At AMIT, Israel has become my home away from home as I am enjoying our amazing tiyulim at the Dead Sea, Ein Gedi, and Zichron Yaakov plus our fun Shabbatonim all over the country. With inspiring chesed trips and volunteering opportunities, I am experiencing Israel in a way that I never have before."

—Malka

MIDRESHET EIN HANATZIV TCI

https://www.midrasha.co.il/seminar
Esther Fisher • esterf45@gmail.com
midresheteinhanatziv@gmail.com

Description of Program:

Do you want to get to know Israel, learn significant Torah, be part of a great group of students, and also deal with questions of society and Jewish identity? Midreshet Ein Hanatziv's TCI program offers you these and much more.

Length of Program:

Please contact for more details

Location of Program:

Beit Shean Valley

Supervision:

Esther Fisher, esterf45@gmail.com

Cost Range:

Please contact for more details

- **What are living arrangements like:** Please contact for more details
- **# of Meals:** Please contact for more details
- **Trips:** Please contact for more details
- **Any other activities or accommodations included in cost:** Please contact for more details
- **Additional add on (that can affect cost):** Please contact for more details

MIDRESHET EIN HANATZIV TCI

(Continued)

Religious Observance and/or Program Philosophy:

Modern Orthodox

Program Highlights:

- Kibbutz life
- Community events
- Learning styles designed specifically for each student

MIDRESHET EMUNAH V'OMANUT

http://www.emunahvomanut.org
Rabbi David Debow • ddebow@emunah.org

Description of Program:

Emunah v'Omanut strives to help its students live inspired religious lives. Through the development of multiple modalities—mind, heart and expression—students can bring all of their youthful vitality into the service of Hashem. Thus we stress developing our minds through Torah study, our creative capacity through artistic expression, emotional depth through reflective study in a nurturing environment, and a vibrant appreciation of G-d's wondrous world through a developed aesthetic sense.

Length of Program:

9.5 months; September to June

Location of Program:

Jerusalem

Supervision:

Please contact for more details

Cost Range:

$29,400

- **What are living arrangements like:** University dorms
- **# of Meals:** Please contact for more details
- **Trips:** Please contact for more details
- **Any other activities or accommodations included in cost:** Please contact for more details

MIDRESHET EMUNAH V'OMANUT

(Continued)

- **Additional add on (that can affect cost):** Please contact for more details

Religious Observance and/or Program Philosophy:

We are a religious Zionist program.

Program Highlights:

- Community service initiatives
- Insightful Torah learning classes
- Creative education

MIDRESHET ESHEL

office@midresheteshel.org • Israel phone: +972-2-966-6621

Description of Program:

Midreshet Eshel is a post-high school seminary that provides young women with a comprehensive educational program emphasizing excellence in Jewish studies, Jewish values, and experiential learning. As the first Sephardic seminary in Israel, Eshel also emphasizes Sephardic *halacha*, customs, and history. The one-year study program combines textual learning with stimulating discussion of topics that are relevant to your life and enhance personal and religious growth.

Length of Program:

9.5 months, September to June

Location of Program:

Jerusalem

Supervision:

Please contact for more details

Cost Range:

$28,000

- **What are living arrangements like:** Rented apartments
- **# of Meals:** Please contact for more details
- **Trips:** Please contact for more details
- **Any other activities or accommodations included in cost:** Please contact for more details

MIDRESHET ESHEL

(Continued)

- **Additional add on (that can affect cost):** Please contact for more details

Religious Observance and/or Program Philosophy:

Orthodox

MIDRESHET HAROVA

harova.org
office@harova.org

Description of Program:

The type of student who is generally attracted to the Midrasha is a highly motivated young woman who is looking for an intensive, high-level program in a strongly Zionist environment. The international character of the student body attracts young women who are interested in interacting with people from different backgrounds and are seeking a less homogeneous atmosphere. The open intellectual environment, combined with the wide variety of the faculty is particularly attractive to a more creative type of student who is interested in exploring a range of ideas and approaches. With more than eighty classes to choose from, students are able to explore any area of Jewish Studies that interests them.

Length of Program:

Full year

Location of Program:

Old City, Jerusalem

Supervision:

Close supervision and support provided by faculty advisors as well as madrichot.

Cost Range:

Tuition includes all classes, full room and board, and health and personal effects insurance. Air fare, as well as an optional trip to Poland are not included in tuition costs.

MIDRESHET HAROVA

(Continued)

- **What are living arrangements like:** Please contact for more details
- **# of Meals:** Please contact for more details
- **Trips**: Please contact for more details
- **Any other activities or accommodations included in cost:** Please contact for more details
- **Additional add on (that can affect cost):** Please contact for more details

Religious Observance and/or Program Philosophy:

Strongly religious Zionist

Program Highlights:

- International environment
- Strongly Religious Zionist
- Wide choices of classes
- Old City location

MIDRESHET LINDENBAUM

https://www.midreshet-lindenbaum.org.il
ml@ots.org.il

Description of Program:

We believe that true religious growth must be based on understanding. The Maria and Joel Finkle Overseas Program at Midreshet Lindenbaum provides the combination of a rigorous, challenging learning program and a supportive religious environment that encourages students to develop and to delve, to discuss and to debate, and ultimately to decide on a more mature and profound commitment to Torah and Mitzvot.

An administration that is open, approachable, and honest sets a standard of integrity and honesty that students learn to match. The academic and personal expectations of a Lindenbaum student are very high. At the end of the year a Midreshet Lindenbaum student will have a deeper commitment to Torat Yisrael, a stronger connection to Eretz Yisrael, and a greater love of Am Yisrael.

Length of Program:

8 months

Location of Program:

Arnona, Jerusalem, Israel

Supervision:

Counselors

Cost Range:

Please contact for more details

- **What are living arrangements like:** Dorm
- **# of Meals:** Three meals a day
- **Trips:** Multiple trips included
- **Any other activities or accommodations included in cost:** Please contact for more details
- **Additional add on (that can affect cost):** Please contact for more details

Religious Observance and/or Program Philosophy:

Modern Orthodox, kosher, Shomer Shabbat

Program Highlights:

- High level Gemara learning
- Great teachers
- Amazing location

Student Highlights:

- Eilat trip
- Yom Kippur

MIDRESHET MORIAH

www.midreshetmoriah.com
midreshetoffice@gmail.com • +972-2-652-7449

Description of Program:

Midreshet Moriah educates toward fear of Heaven; love of Torah, its *mitzvot*, and its values; develops a sense of mission, responsibility, and love for the Jewish people, its destiny, its holy Land, and its State; while focusing on the unique needs and talents of each and every student and aspiring toward continual improvement, educational creativity, and pedagogic excellence.

Length of Program:

Academic year (September to June)

Location of Program:

Baka neighborhood in Jerusalem

Supervision:

Behavior consistent with spending a year in Israel learning Torah (full details in our Student Handbook).

Cost Range:

$30,000

- **What are living arrangements like:** Students live two in a room in apartments of three rooms
- **# of Meals:** Three
- **Trips:** Frequent fun, educational trips, and hikes
- **Any other activities or accommodations included in cost:** Shabbatons, special programs; health insurance included.

MIDRESHET MORIAH

(Continued)

- **Additional add on (that can affect cost):** Please contact for more details

Religious Observance and/or Program Philosophy:

Modern Orthodox

Program Highlights:

- The incredible breadth of amazing course choices
- The most exciting, warm teachers
- Amazing location and facility

Student Highlights:

Variety of classes, teachers are so interested in building connections and having meaningful conversations. You don't live where you learn and there's a beautiful walk in between.

MIDRESHET TEHILLAH

midreshettehillah.nevey.org

rjeremykagan@yahoo.com

Description of Program:

At Midreshet Tehillah, students develop a sensitivity to the depth, subtlety, and complexity of Torah. We engage sources from Tanach (scriptures), Talmud (commentary), Halacha (law), Midrash (stories), and Jewish philosophy to gain a nuanced understanding of their underlying issues and implications. Our students come to appreciate that, rather than a collection of insights, Torah presents us with a powerful, integrated vision of reality and self which transforms our world.

At Midreshet Tehillah we guide each student to grow religiously in a manner structured to her individual character, strengths, and needs while enhancing her self-awareness, self-respect, and sensitivity to others.

Length of Program:

9 months

Location of Program:

Har Noff, Jerusalem

Supervision:

Check with school for specifics

Cost Range:

$25,000

- **What are living arrangements like:** Dorms
- **# of Meals:** Three
- **Trips:** Once a month

MIDRESHET TEHILLAH

(Continued)

- **Any other activities or accommodations included in cost:** Please contact for more details
- **Additional add on (that can affect cost):** Please contact for more details

Religious Observance and/or Program Philosophy:

Orthodox

Program Highlights:

- Diversity of the girls: US, UK, Mexico, Australia, Canada, etc.
- Tracks
- *Tehillah Track*: lively classroom-based interactive lecture/discussion format.
- *Beit Midrash Track:* a chavruta (partner study hall independent type) format.
- Tiyulim and Shabbatonim (trips and Shabbat experience); there are many occasions throughout the year that students get to tune into the special vibe of the place or the day.

MIDRESHET TORAT CHESSED

Shira Melamed • office@mtcstaff.com • +972-52-436-5031

Description of Program:

MTC believes that authentic and long-lasting growth comes from combining learning Torah with the act of chesed. At MTC you will have the once-in-a-lifetime opportunity to combine your days with engaging, thought-provoking, and exciting classes given by an incredible staff of teachers and genuine chesed. After a morning of learning, and delving deeper into their Jewish roots, our students spend their afternoons with their kids from Bet Elazraki Children's Home. They become mentors and best friends to children, and our students change for the better as a result every single day. In addition to incredible day-to-day activities and classes, MTC has numerous tiyulim and shabbatonim all over Israel, connecting you on a deeper level to your heritage and your country.

Length of Program:

Academic year

Location of Program:

Netanya, Israel (seven minute walk from the beach)

Supervision:

Our students live in houses with a madricha in each house. All MTC administrators live walking distance from the dorms as well. There are rules that our students must respect in order to participate in our program.

Cost Range:

Contact office

- **What are living arrangements like:** Our students live in beautiful houses with a fully equipped kitchen, laundry room, backyard, and wifi.
- **# of Meals:** Three
- **Trips:** MTC takes its students on numerous tiyulim and seminars around the country throughout the year.
- **Any other activities or accommodations included in cost:** MTC covers transportation to Jerusalem so that our students can visit their friends when they are off.
- **Additional add on (that can affect cost):** Please contact for more details

Religious Observance and/or Program Philosophy:

Modern Orthodox

Program Highlights:

- With so many different classes there's something for everyone.
- You will become a role model, mentor, and friend to children who are in need of love.
- Travel the land and watch your learning come alive.

Student Highlights:

"The entire environment at MTC is life changing to say the least. Each individual class teaches so much about what it is like to be a Jew in today's society and how to grow into the best us we can be. I don't think I have ever had so much inspiration in such a short span of time and I could not be any more grateful for having been given this opportunity."

—Pessi

MIDRESHET TORAT CHESSED

(Continued)

"MTC has played a critical role in deepening my Jewish identity and sense of self through our diverse classes and teachers who serve as phenomenal role models. Beyond the learning, MTC has strengthened my love of working with kids and my sense of community. My kids have become my pride and joy, my peers, my best friends, and MTC has truly become home."
  —Shira

"MTC is the first place where I've been able to learn about what's important in the morning and then live it in the afternoons—every single day. There's a special sense of accomplishment in using your year, not only to better yourself, but to also take what you've been working on and put it to use."
  —Orly

MIDRESHET TORAH V'AVODAH (MTVA)

MTVAIsrael.org
office@tvaisrael.org • Israel line: 0507098304 / US line in Israel: 646-248-7555 • US office: 212-465-9536

Description of Program:

Midreshet Torah v'Avodah is an innovative Bnei Akiva midrasha for highly motivated high school graduates. It is the first midrasha to offer a truly integrated experience. In one incredible year, you will experience life-changing growth in your connection to Torah, to the Jewish people, and to the land and State of Israel. You will have the opportunity to learn from the most impressive educators in today's religious Zionist community. Because we believe that learning in Israel must extend outside the four walls of the beit-midrash, we embark on many amazing tiyulim, weekly volunteering, a week of teaching English in a development town, two weeks on a Religious Zionist kibbutz, Poland journey, Ulpan and many Shabbatonim in communities throughout the country. MTVA's path-breaking model allows you to expand and broaden every aspect of who you are as a member of Am Yisrael in Medinat Yisrael through the lens of Torat Eretz Yisrael.

Length of Program:

10 months

Location of Program:

Katamon, Jerusalem

Supervision:

Madrichot and some staff members live on campus, and the Eym-Bayit and her family lives in an apartment adjacent to the campus. Everyone

MIDRESHET TORAH V'AVODAH (MTVA)

(Continued)

is expected to interact with students, staff, society, and Hashem with the highest degree of respect at all times.

Cost Range:

$32,000

- **What are living arrangements like:** Our dorms are located in a closed campus, in the same building as the beit-midrash, class-rooms, dining room and lounges. Each dorm apartment has a fully equipped kitchen.
- **# of Meals:** Two to three daily
- **Trips:** Many! Many tiyulim throughout the country. Shabbatonim in various communities throughout the country approximately every other Shabbat. One week of service-learning in a development town in southern Israel, two weeks on a Religious-Zionist kibbutz, Poland journey.
- **Any other activities or accommodations included in cost:** All trips included in cost, except Poland
- **Additional add on (that can affect cost):** Medical insurance is not included in the cost

Religious Observance and/or Program Philosophy:

Religious Zionist

Program Highlights:

- Unbelievably caring, devoted, and charismatic staff

MIDRESHET TORAH V'AVODAH (MTVA)

(Continued)

- Innovative approach to Torah learning which fosters life-long love of Torah and preparation for life as a Torah-observant Jew after the year in Israel
- Engagement with Eretz Yisrael, Am Yisrael, and Torat Yisrael

Student Highlights:

- *Our Shabbatot:* unique and distinct locations that aren't classic to other seminary experiences. For example, we were taken to Bnai Brak one Shabbat and to Tel Aviv the following Shabbat to compare diverse cultures and understand respect of all perspectives of Judaism.
- *World Renowned Teachers:* not only are they well respected teachers within the greater Jewish community but they take the time to get to know you personally. TVA thrives by having panels often that represent widespread different halachik opinions.
- *The people:* TVA prides themselves on recruiting top Jewish leaders of tomorrow. They do it so meticulously that the group dynamic is incomparable and unparalleled. Whether it be religious background or from within the tri state vs anywhere else in the country, every girl who walks through the doors is valued.

NISHMAT

www.nishmat.net
info@nishmat.net • Phone: +972-2-640-4339 • Direct US Line to
Israel office: 212-444-1988 • Fax: +972-2-640-4353

Description of Program:

At Nishmat you will spend a year studying in chevruta, side-by side with
Nishmat's advanced scholars, in our Bet Midrash. You will develop profi-
ciency in Tanach, Gemara, Halacha, and Machshava.

You will be integrated into an Israel Bet Midrash sharing your chevrutot,
classes and dormitory apartments with Israeli students—b'Ivrit.

At Nishmat, growth in Avodat Hashem comes through learning Torah
and through sharing Shabbatot, tefillah, and chesed together with an exceptional community of students and faculty. With shiurim on Chassidut,
Tefillah, Mussar and Machashava, we encourage each student to fulfill
her spiritual potential, to embark on a lifelong journey of Torah study and
worship of G-d.

Length of Program:

August to June

Location of Program:

Pat Neighborhood, Jerusalem
Jerusalem 9328249

Supervision:

When interviewing and processing applications we look for responsible,
independent students who have a sense of responsibility to their learning
program and arrive back at the dormitory at reasonable times. Due to the
high ratio of staff to students, the madrichot, the director, and the staff are

able to keep track of the activities of each student. All alcohol and drugs are strictly forbidden to students under any circumstances. Curfew: 12:30 a.m.

Cost Range:

Tuition & Dormitory: $26,500 (includes tuition, medical insurance, extra-curricular activities, accommodation, and hot lunch)

- **What are living arrangements like:** Nishmat students live in dormitory apartments on a closed campus that includes the Bet Midrash and classrooms. Apartments accommodate five to six students. The typical bedroom is furnished with beds, closet space, chairs, and desks for two students. The common area consists of a living area, a kitchen (supplied with stovetop, refrigerator, dairy and parve dishes and utensils), a bathroom. The campus maintains coin operated washing machines and dryers, as well as an elliptical machine and treadmill.
- **# of Meals:** One (lunch)
- **Trips:** Every month students leave Jerusalem at least once, with hiking boots and a Tanach, and explore the country. The other monthly tiyul is one in a series of "siyurim" in and around Jerusalem. Students learn about the neighborhoods of Old and New Jerusalem, the history, the synagogues, and the personalities that have made Jerusalem what it is.
- **Any other activities or accommodations included in cost:** Please contact for more details
- **Additional add on (that can affect cost):** Please contact for more details

NISHMAT

Religious Observance and/or Program Philosophy:

Modern Orthodox

Program Highlights:

- We are prepared to consider special requests from students with special interests: we have had students who also are musicians, athletes, volunteers at MDA, and even a volunteer firefighter. All students participate in chesed activities, volunteering with various organizations in Jerusalem, tutoring, and assisting needy families.
- Uniquely in Shana Ba'Aretz, you will enjoy your own program as well as be fully integrated with your Israeli counterparts. Students take two-thirds of their classes together with Israeli students, and one third by themselves. Most classes are Ivrit b'Ivrit; you may also choose from a variety of English-language classes in Nishmat's Alisa Flatow Overseas Program.

SHA'ALVIM FOR WOMEN

www.shaalvim.org/sfw
Rabbi Yamin Goldsmith • Email: sfw.shaalvim@gmail.com
Phone: (02) 678-4062

Description of Program:

At Sha'alvim for women we strive for our students to…

a. Continue and enhance their love for learning Torah.

b. Engage their minds, their hearts, and their souls in their personal growth and in their Torah study.

c. Grow with and from the kindness and sincerity of each member of our exceptional staff along with the individual attention provided to each student.

d. Continue and enhance their development of Middot.

e. Develop further in their yirat shamayim, ahavat HaShem, derech eretz, and avodah shebalev (tefilah).

f. Expand upon their Torah learning skills that they will take with them beyond their "year in Israel."

g. Develop a deep appreciation for and a sense of obligation to their family, their school, and their community.

h. Expand their love for Am Yisra'el, Eretz Yisra'el, and Medinat Yisra'el. Our unique, integrated program of shiurim and siyurim, together with our extended tiyulim and meaningful, outstanding programs on Yom HaAtzmaut, Yom Yerushalayim, and through-out the year expand our students' love for the Land, the People, and the State of Israel.

Length of Program:

September to June

SHA'ALVIM FOR WOMEN

(Continued)

Location of Program:

Malcha, Jerusalem

Supervision:

Safety and security are very important to us. Curfew is strictly enforced and attendance is taken in every class. Students are expected to conduct themselves at all times in a manner befitting bnot Torah.

Cost Range:

$28,850

- **What are living arrangements like:** Hotel layout building with several mini apartments—four girls in each (two rooms so two girls per apartment).

  Living Quarters:
  Comfortable dormitory, laundry service, twenty-four-hour security, dorms open all time (i.e. every Shabbat, Sukkot, Chanuka, Pesach, etc.).

  Availability of Private Kitchen Facilities:
  The kitchenette facilities include refrigerators, microwave, and toasters.

- **# of Meals:** Three
- **Trips:** Our students have the unique opportunity to study about a wide variety of locations in Israel and then, using maps, a Tanach, and relevant history books, go and visit the very places they studied. In this way, they re-enact thousands of years of our history, from the Tanach to Modern Israel, in an unparalleled hands-on

program. At the end of the year, we can look back at a map and feel unbelievably accomplished as we see how we made the locations of the Chumash, Navi, Mishna, Gmara, Rishonim, Acharonim, and modern heroes come to life. In addition, three times a year, we at SFW pack our bags and visit major sections of the country on overnight tiyulim. We hike the North, the South, and the Tzfat area until we drop, visiting major and minor sites and getting to know our faculty (who join us), our friends, and our country in a different setting. In addition to these major excursions, we have a number of day-long tiyulim to places such as Masada and Caesarea.

- **Any other activities or accommodations included in cost:** Please contact for more details
- **Additional add on (that can affect cost):** Please contact for more details

Religious Observance and/or Program Philosophy:

Modern Orthodox

TIFERET

http://www.tiferetcenter.com
info@tiferetcenter.com • 02-999-7957

Description of Program:

Tiferet is a Religious-Zionist school that aims to give its students an all-encompassing Israel experience that appeals to the mind, body, and soul. We aspire to enlighten our students and broaden their understanding and knowledge of Judaism, as well as inspire them toward a closer connection to Torah, Am Yisrael, Eretz Yisrael, and Medinat Yisrael.

Our objective is to create an experience that maximizes all that the year in Israel has to offer. With a beautiful new campus in a close-knit community, we have created a warm and comfortable environment where our students can focus on learning, growing, and making incredible relationships that will last a lifetime.

Length of Program:

Academic year

Location of Program:

Ramat Beit Shemesh Alef

Supervision:

Please contact for more details

Cost Range:

Contact program.

- **What are living arrangements like:** Please contact for more details
- **# of Meals:** Please contact for more details
- **Trips:** Please contact for more details

- **Any other activities or accommodations included in cost:** Please contact for more details
- **Additional add on (that can affect cost):** Please contact for more details

Religious Observance and/or Program Philosophy:

Zionistic

Program Highlights:

- *Relationships*: In a short time, you will develop strong and lifetime relationships with the same teachers that are inspiring you in the classroom. All of our teachers make time to meet and learn with you individually. Our warm environment helps you acclimate easily—no waiting until December to start getting into it.
- *Learning*: Because your teachers know your name and you've been to their house for a Shabbat meal several times, you will feel very comfortable in the classroom. Since each teacher knows each of their students so well, there is no need for mandatory tests and exams—class is stress-free. Optional tests are offered for review purposes only.
- *Your home away from home*: You will never have the pressure of finding a place to go for Shabbat, Sukkot, or Pesach—you are always welcome to stay in Tiferet and go to your teachers for meals. We have Rosh Hashana and Yom Kippur davening in our Bet Midrash and you enjoy your meals with your teachers. You don't need to find a place to go! Some of the most memorable moments in a yeshiva is davening with your friends and teachers on Rosh Hashana and Yom Kippur and spending your Purim Seuda with

TIFERET

your Rebbeim. At Tiferet, you have those memorable experiences as well! We have a brand new and beautiful campus that was built specifically for your needs.

Student Highlights:

"I spent my Gap Year at Tiferet Center in Ramat Beit Shemesh. Something that really sets Tiferet apart is its location. We are RBS with our teachers just around the corner from us, if we ever need them, they are only a few minutes away. Something unique about Tiferet is that they are always open to their students through the whole year. We are never forced to find somewhere else to go for holidays or shabbat. Lastly, the relationships we get the opportunity to build with our teachers is incredible. The effort they put into ensuring we feel we are a part of a family is unmatched. They really do give us a home away from home."

 —Leorah

TORAH TECH (WOMENS)

TorahTech.co
Info@TorahTech.co • +1-914-336-4313

Description of Program:

Torah Tech is a unique gap-year program in Israel for young adults that integrates intensive Torah study with professional development through business and tech internships. Our multifaceted program challenges students to strive for excellence both religiously and professionally, by immersing them in the world of Torah and ruchniyut, as well as the world of high-powered Israeli businesses and tech companies. This rare combination can only be found in Eretz Yisrael, the eternal homeland of Am Yisrael and the birthplace of unparalleled innovation and advancement in business and technology.

Students will also connect to the land of Israel through exciting trips and tours, give back to the community through chesed projects and volunteer work, hear from distinguished religious personalities from both the Torah and corporate worlds, and enjoy exclusive access to nearby gyms, beaches, self defense training courses, and much more. The result? Students who will have developed into passionate, independent, and empowered young adults with the necessary tools to succeed as bnei Torah in the modern world. At Torah Tech, you won't just learn Torah, you'll live it.

Length of Program:

9 months

Location of Program:

Ranana

TORAH TECH (WOMENS)

(Continued)

Supervision:

Our post-high school Gap Year program is meant for mature, responsible, and passionate young women who genuinely seek to deepen their connection to God, Israel, and the Jewish people through intensive Torah study and authentic, real-life modern Israel. Students should be both highly motivated to, as well as capable of, living independently, growing religiously, and succeed both academically and in a workplace environment. Visit our website for staff information.

Cost Range:

Please contact for more details.

- **What are living arrangements like:** Torah Tech Womens is located in Tel Aviv, the heart of central Israel and the home of start-up nation. Students will live in several apartments inside the city, each equipped with a kitchen, several full bathrooms, and living areas. Daily Torah study will take place in a centrally located Beit Midrash. Students will enjoy easy access to public transportation, close proximity to gyms, synagogues, beaches, museums, and malls, and the unique opportunity to experience life in modern Israel first-hand.
- **# of Meals:** Three meals a day
- **Trips:** See all of ancient and modern Israel. From hikes through caves to conferences featuring top Israeli investors, you'll connect to the past, present, and future of our homeland and our people.
- **Any other activities or accommodations included in cost:** With options for gym membership, krav maga army training, biking,

surfing, volleyball, basketball, baseball, our students are constantly active. Beaches offer the perfect setting for down time as well.

- **Additional add on (that can affect cost):** Please contact for more details

Religious Observance and/or Program Philosophy:

Orthodox. We aim to deliver knowledge, tools, and once-in-a-lifetime experiences to our students so they can discover their religious identity and purpose, build their professional future, and be fully prepared to succeed in the next stages of life.

Program Highlights:

- Learning from professionals
- Personal attention
- High level internships

MEN'S PROGRAMS

AISH GESHER

www.aishgesher.com

egreene@aish.com • 1-914-775-5206

Description of Program:

Aish Gesher is everything you're looking for in a yeshiva! If you're looking for great learning, we've got it. If you're looking for warm rabbis, they are right here. If you want an awesome group of serious, but fun guys, that's our chevre. If you're looking for Jewish philosophy, we're the experts. If you're looking for a spiritual environment, you can't get better than across from the Kotel. If you're looking for a comfortable facility, our campus is it. If you're looking to meet new, interesting people, our Beis Midrash is filled with them.

If you're looking to use your year in Israel to the max, conquering both mountains and Masechtas, we will make it happen. Aish is synonymous with authentic spirituality, great learning, and building leaders for the Jewish people. In a warm and nurturing environment, we will help you become the best you, and the best Jew, you can be.

Length of Program:

September to June

Location of Program:

Old City, Jerusalem

Supervision:

Students are supervised by administration and staff in all realms of their student life. Rabbis are available all day. Dedicated dorm counselors (madrichim) live and learn with them daily. Curfew is 12 a.m., ensuring students are safe and secure. An on-campus medical clinic provides for health needs.

AISH GESHER

Cost Range:

Please contact for details.

- **What are living arrangements like:** The dormitory has AC in every room. Most rooms are four people per room. Brand new showers, workout room, recreation room. Cleaned twice a week.
- **# of Meals:** Three meals a day
- **Trips:** Often and awesome
- **Any other activities or accommodations included in cost:** All included other than the list below.
- **Additional add on (that can affect cost):** Flights, insurance ($1.50 a day), books, spending on travel plans for Shabbat, etc.

Religious Observance and/or Program Philosophy:

Aish Gesher is an Orthodox program. The broader Aish HaTorah yeshiva welcomes all Jews and the environment is one of tolerance, brotherhood, and religious growth.

Program Highlights:

- The unique expertise of our Rabbis in Jewish philosophy and spirituality.
- The warmth and love shown to the students. The rabbis and their families treat the students like family.
- Location can't be beat. Heart of the Old City, across from the Kotel. The Old City is a rich place to live for a year and develop one's deeper connection to Judaism.

DERECH ETZ CHAIM

Rabbi Aharon Katz • office@ondec.net • 972-2-654-1379

Description of Program:

Derech Etz Chaim, as the name implies, is about helping Talmidim see Torah as "Life." To encourage them to think, and see Avodas Hashem as the focal point of who they are. To help them develop into independent thinkers, who will fearlessly ask questions and search for answers while being deeply committed to Torah growth and learning.

The yeshiva offers close guidance on a continual course of advancement that incorporates Torah as a means for individual development. Through a close kesher (connection) with your Rebbeim, coupled with a dynamic learning environment and small classes, you will lay the foundation upon which your future learning will firmly stand.

We want our students to ask questions. The learning day is interwoven with Shiurim focusing on asking the "Why" behind Mitzvos and Avodas Hashem, and encouraging our Talmidim to think about their lives and the direction in which they wish it to endure.

Length of Program:

August to June

Location of Program:

Har nof, Jerusalem

Supervision:

Rabbi Aharon Katz; can be contacted at: rak@ondec.net

Cost Range:

$25,500, includes everything

DERECH ETZ CHAIM

(Continued)

- **What are living arrangements like:** University dorms
- **# of Meals:** Please contact for more details
- **Trips:** Please contact for more details
- **Any other activities or accommodations included in cost:** Please contact for more details
- **Additional add on (that can affect cost):** Please contact for more details

Religious Observance and/or Program Philosophy:

Orthodox

Program Highlights:

- First year Talmidim at Derech Etz Chaim participate monthly in group volunteer programs around Israel with organizations like Yad Eliezer, One Family (for victims of terror), Leket Israel, Shalva, and others.
- The yeshiva also has a monthly Israel advocacy class to familiarize our Talmidim with the current issues and challenges that Klal Yisrael and the State of Israel face.
- Derech Etz Chaim is well known for its powerhouse teams in the American Flag Football League in Israel. The yeshiva also participates in the basketball and softball leagues and provides a weight room, and an outdoor basketball court as well as an indoor gym for basketball for our students to use.

DERECH OHR SAMEACH

http://www.derechinstitute.com/
Israel Office • Rabbi Nachy Brickman / Jonathan Speculand
derech@ohr.edu • Phone: (02) 581-8325 • Fax: (02) 636-9100

Description of Program:

Derech's approach is based on the verse, "Chanoch lanaar al pi darko" (Mishlei 22:6, "Educate a child according to his unique qualities"). Every student is treated as an individual, and no singular educational approach works best with every individual. There are many legitimate ways to serve Hashem. Some of our graduates continue learning in kollel while others join the Israeli army. Most return to North America, Europe, or South Africa for university or vocational school. We work with students to help them identify their strengths and talents, nurture these in the course of their studies, and try to give them skills to implement them in the future so that they can become productive members of their Jewish communities.

Length of Program:

September to June

Location of Program:

22 Shimon Hatzadik Street, Jerusalem

Supervision:

Type of American Student: A wide range, including students with a strong yeshiva background usually looking to strengthen their hashkafos, Modern Orthodox, Chassidic, and Yeshivishe, as well as students who recently became religious.

DERECH OHR SAMEACH

(Continued)

Cost Range:

Tuition for the academic year is $22,500. There are a number of sources for scholarships and financial aid that we work with regularly.

- **What are living arrangements like:** Please contact for more details
- **# of Meals:** Please contact for more details
- **Trips:** Please contact for more details
- **Any other activities or accommodations included in cost:** Please contact for more details
- **Additional add on (that can affect cost):** Please contact for more details

Religious Observance and/or Program Philosophy:

Orthodox

Program Highlights:

- We run chesed activities like serving in a soup kitchen and volunteering in old age homes.
- Work-out room, game room, local soccer and basketball courts, rented gyms and pools.
- Tiyulim around the entire country, including visits to holy cities and locations, hiking, crawling through Bar Kochva caves, and boating on the Kineret.

DVAR YERUSHALAYIM

http://www.dvar.org.il
Katzenellenbogen 53, PO Box 34580 Har Nof, Jerusalem, 91344
dvar@dvar.org.il • Phone: (02) 652-2817 • Fax: (02) 652-2827

Description of Program:

Our yeshiva is one of the first yeshiva to cater to Jewish students with limited backgrounds in Torah Learning. The Academy designed a unique professional introduction to the source-material of Torah in order to facilitate successful study by beginning students.

Length of Program:

Contact office for schedule

Location of Program:

Har Nof Jerusalem
91344 Israel

Supervision:

Please reach out for more details

Cost Range:

Monthly tuition, including dorm and meals, is $1,500. Call for details.

- **What are living arrangements like:** Please reach out for more details
- **# of Meals:** Please reach out for more details
- **Trips:** Please reach out for more details
- **Any other activities or accommodations included in cost:** Please reach out for more details
- **Additional add on (that can affect cost):** Please reach out for more details

DVAR YERUSHALAYIM

(Continued)

Religious Observance and/or Program Philosophy:

Orthodox

Program Highlights:

- We have a special one-year program, accredited by Touro and other US colleges, for post high school graduates and post 6th formers. Masa Fellowship program.
- Classes in English, Hebrew, Russian, French; individually-tailored curricula; training in independent study; academic and personal counseling; part-time and summer courses; Kollel and Research Department; Kiruv and Semicha program; Daily Ulpan; audio visual programs and distant teaching; tours of historic sites; and college credits.

HAKOTEL

https://www.hakotel.org.il • office@hakotel.org.il

Description of Program:

The yeshiva's underlying goal is to cultivate an intimate connection to Torat Yisrael, Am Yisrael, Eretz Yisrael. Developing a talmid's love for learning, bond with Eretz Yisrael, and sense of responsibility towards Am Yisrael are the yeshiva's primary objectives.

Length of Program:

The majority go for two years.

Location of Program:

Old City Jerusalem

Supervision:

Yeshivat Hakotel accepts only fully motivated boys. We assume a high level of seriousness and maturity. Alcohol and substance abuse as well as other conduct not befitting a ben Torah are grounds for immediate dismissal. We do not have a curfew, but ask boys to notify a madrich when leaving so that we can ensure each individual's safety.

Cost Range:

$26,500, room and board

- **What are living arrangements like:** The dormitories consist of apartments of three bedrooms each with three to four boys per room. Each apartment has bathroom and shower facilities. Because of our goal of integration, Israeli and overseas students share rooms. A washing machine and dryer are available for student use.

- **# of Meals:** Three
- **Trips:** To further enhance our Tanach shiurim as well as to promote yediat ha-aretz, the yeshiva offers monthly half-day tiyulim. All tiyulim are army approved and in accordance with security regulations. The yeshiva organizes two major tiyulim during bein hazmanim to the North and South.
- **Any other activities or accommodations included in cost:** Tiyulim
- **Additional add on (that can affect cost):** Poland trip

Religious Observance and/or Program Philosophy:

Full commitment to shmirat Torah U'mitzvot is a prerequisite. Our stringent entrance requirements assure that students are motivated to learn and develop both personally and spiritually.

Program Highlights:

- Having the Poland trip early in the year really sets a tone of seriousness in Avodat Hashem from the beginning.
- The yeshiva pushes for us to open our Hashkafic wordview, and being in the Old City helps initiate that growth due to the diversity around us. For example, the yeshiva pushes us to spend Yat Kislev at the big Lubavitcher Kollel right nearby.
- The responsibility that is placed on the shoulders of the Shana Daled guys truly makes for a family-like environment.

Student Highlights:

"My year at HaKotel was one I'll never forget. Not only did I grow exponentially in learning, but I really cultivated a relationship with Eretz Yisroel."

- "Yeshivat HaKotel offered me the supportive learning environment that has helped me become who I am today."
- "The Rabbonim and staff at yeshiva treated me like family from day one and pushed me to be my best. I will cherish those bonds forever."

HAR ETZION

Yeshivat Har Etzion
Alon Shevut, Gush Etzion 90433
Eli Weber • Eli.weber5@gmail.com • office@etzion.org.il
(P) 972-2-993-7300 • (F) 972-2-993-1298

Description of Program:

The goal of the yeshiva is to foster within the talmidim a deeper and fuller life of Avodat Hashem. The yeshiva emphasizes Talmud Torah as a vital and indispensable instrument for a relationship with the Kadosh Baruch Hu. To cultivate an authentic love for Torah, a talmid must be equipped with the tools and skills to master its learning. The yeshiva excels at imparting the systematic and organized method of learning known to many as the "Brisker style" of learning.

A Ben Torah embraces the challenges of our society, ennobling both his own personal experience as well as his environment. The road to religious and personal depth is paved with healthy "struggle;" by acknowledging the complexity of Avodat Hashem and the diversity among different types of Bnei Torah, a person can assure the emergence of an authentic and passionate religious identity. Level of learning offered is advanced and participants are to be able to independently study a Talmudic passage and an advanced knowledge of Hebrew is required as shiurim are mainly in Hebrew

Length of Program:

August to June

Location of Program:

Alon shevut

Supervision:

Please contact for more details

197

HAR ETZION

Cost Range:

$23,000 USD. This includes dormitory, meals, and laundry service.

- **What are living arrangements like:** Please contact for more details
- **# of Meals:** Please contact for more details
- **Trips:** Please contact for more details
- **Any other activities or accommodations included in cost:** Please contact for more details
- **Additional add on (that can affect cost):** Please contact for more details

Religious Observance and/or Program Philosophy:

Orthodox. A full commitment to shmirat Torah U'mitzvot is a prerequisite

Program Highlights:

- *Interaction with Israelis:* Interaction with Israeli students is enthusiastically encouraged. Talmidim are offered the opportunity to room with Israelis, learn with Israeli chevrutot and ultimately, to transfer to an Israeli shiur. The language of the shiurim (Hebrew), the relatively small number of overseas students, and the common schedule assures that overseas talmidim will feel an integrated part of the overall yeshiva. Shabbatot Iruach are dedicated to heightening this feeling. Group discussions between overseas students and Israelis, joint tischim, and Shabbatot in which each American is invited to an Israeli talmid's home, all contribute to a strong bond. Though students are encouraged to remain informed of Israeli society, no special emphasis is placed upon politics. The staff is careful not to distract the talmid's Torah focus with political agendas or to indoctrinate personal political views.

- *Sports Facilities:* For recreation, there is an array of indoor and outdoor sports facilities within a five-minute walk of the yeshiva, including a gym, weight room, and an indoor swimming pool.

- *Special Informal Programs:* Throughout the year, special guest speakers visit the yeshiva. Some address the entire Yeshiva while others speak to the smaller group of overseas talmidim. These speakers encourage talmidim to grapple with relevant and contemporary issues. Festive yeshiva-wide Chagigot take place on Chanuka, Purim, Yom Ha'atzmaut and Yom Yerushalayim. Smaller chagigot for the overseas group or particular shiurim are also scheduled on these occasions.

KEREM B'YAVNEH

www.kby.org
Rav David Zahtz • il@kby.org.il • 052-6164216
US #: 9178095295 • Canada #: 6478481736
Whatsapp #: +972526164216

Description of Program:

The yeshiva aims to produce bnei-Torah who combine a high degree of Torah learning, proper observance, and character refinement, and who are able to cope successfully with the modern challenges encountered in their respective professions while contributing to the building of Israel and the strengthening of Diaspora Jewry. The yeshiva's many alumni proudly demonstrate that it is possible to be a ben-Torah with a clear religious outlook in the modern world.

Length of Program:

August to June

Location of Program:

Doar Na Evtach 7985500

Supervision:

Level of Learning Offered
The Yeshiva caters to the advanced talmid, who is able to independently learn a Talmudic passage and also to intermediate students. Additionally, the yeshiva has begun to offer a mechina track for individuals who are extremely motivated and serious but lack experience and knowledge of basic skills.

Hebrew Knowledge Required
Intermediate shiurim are in Hebrew and English.

KEREM B'YAVNEH

(Continued)

Religious Observance Required
A full commitment to shmirat Torah U'mitzvot is a prerequisite.

Cost Range:

$26,500; the fees cover tuition, maintenance, meals, dormitory, laundry, medical and hospitalization insurance, and field trips.

- **What are living arrangements like:** Please reach out for more details
- **# of Meals:** Please reach out for more details
- **Trips:** Please reach out for more details
- **Any other activities or accommodations included in cost:** Please reach out for more details
- **Additional add on (that can affect cost):** Please reach out for more details

Religious Observance and/or Program Philosophy:

Orthodox

Program Highlights:

- *Special Informal Programs:* On most Shabbatot there are Melaveh Malka programs, which often feature guest speakers. Guest speakers are also invited on Chanukah, Yom Ha'atzmaut, Yom Yerushalayim and other special days. There are a number of Yemei Iyun throughout the year, most notably on 7 Adar, the Yahrzeit of founding Rosh Hayeshiva, Maran Harav Chaim Yaakov Goldvicht zt"l.

- *Sports Facilities:* The yeshiva has a basketball court on campus and a weight room, which are open after seder hours. The nearby Givat Washington has a pool, which some talmidim use on Fridays in the summer.
- *Field Trips:* The yeshiva has two major tiyulim during Bein Hazmanim, one to the Galil and one to the Negev. In addition, there are a number of tiyulim on Fridays, often as part of Shabbatonim. The goal of these tiyulim is to develop a connection to Am Yisrael in Eretz Yisrael and to bring to life the setting of the Tanach narrative.

MAYANOT POST HIGH SCHOOL PROGRAM

www.mayanot.edu
office@mayanot.edu

Description of Program:

A Gap Year yeshiva designed for Chabad kids with not such a strong Lubavitch education. The post high school track is one of three tracks Mayanot offers, and it consists of a full day of learning with occasional tiyulim (trips), shabbatons, and volunteering opportunities. Classes are centered around a typical yeshiva schedule, with Talmud, Tanach, and Jewish History with an added emphasis of Chabad Chassidus in those classes.

Length of Program:

Two semesters:

- First semester: Typically from September until mid-January
- Second semester: End of January until June (with most of April off due to Pesach)

Location of Program:

28 David Yellin St, Jerusalem
Short walk away from Machane Yehuda, Ben Yehuda, Meah Shearim, Central Station, and Old City

Supervision:

Please contact for more details

Cost Range:

$22,000

- **What are living arrangements like:** Dorms, with typically three to four per room; you can request roommates.
- **# of Meals:** Three meals a day including Shabbos
- **Trips:** all trips and shabbatons
- **Any other activities or accommodations included in cost:** Please contact for more details
- **Additional add on (that can affect cost):** Please contact for more details

Religious Observance and/or Program Philosophy:

Orthodox (Lubavitch/Chabad)

Program Highlights:

- Small size (around thirty-five students), more individualized schedules and chances to connect with Rabbeim.
- Older Rabbinical students (shluchim) are readily available to learn with outside of class.
- Chabad-styled education complete with regular Farbrengens (get-togethers), as well as opportunities to do chesed.

Student Highlights:

- "I went to Mayanot really detached from Judaism, but through the incredible rabbeim and students the fire within me has been rekindled and I'm more committed as a Jew than ever."
- "The small, yet diverse student population of Mayanot allowed me to become friends with everybody. I now have friends from five different countries and ten different states and I'm closer than

I've ever been with them, despite not being there for a couple of months."

- "I was looking for a yeshiva that wasn't entirely focused on Gemara and Mayanot was the perfect place. Not only are there many different subjects to learn, it actually sparked a love for Gemara within me, something which I would have never dreamed about."

MIGDAL HaTORAH

Rabbi Aryeh Wasserman • info@migdalhatorah.org

Description of Program:

Yeshivat Migdal HaTorah offers a unique experience for post yeshiva high school students. We aim to cultivate a ben-Torah, who excels in all aspects of life. A strong emphasis is placed on in-depth analytical study as well as the development of proper middot. In addition to offering unique, high-level study of Gemara, the Migdal curriculum focuses on Fundamental Jewish Philosophy and contemporary Halacha, targeting the many challenges bnei-Torah will face as they establish careers and confront the complexities of our modern world. The curriculum also has many shiurim focused on the study of Tanach, Halacha, Eretz Yisrael, and forays into topics such as Physics and Socratic Logic. Migdal offers its students an individualized learning program that provides them with the skills needed for independent self-study of the Torah in accordance with the unique method of Rabbi Joseph B. Soloveitchik. Becoming a student at Migdal means being challenged and inspired—there is a high level of analytical thinking, applied to Talmud and philosophy. Knowledge of Hebrew required is minimal as most shiurim are in English.

Length of Program:

September to June

Location of Program:

12 Nachal Paran
Modiin, Israel

Supervision:

Yeshivat Migdal HaTorah seeks motivated students from diverse backgrounds who are committed to serious Torah learning and desire to become independent learners and thinkers. If you are a mature student who is ready to grow, question, and be challenged while enjoying the beauty and wonder of Israel, then Migdal is for you.

Cost Range:

$26,500 USD; this includes room board.

- **What are living arrangements like:** Please reach out for more details
- **# of Meals:** Three meals a day
- **Trips:** Please reach out for more details. The yeshiva feels strongly that trips are a pivotal part of the year in Israel, and sets aside significant time to ensure that the relationship between each student and the land is as strong as possible. Our tiyulim will take students across the length and width of Israel. From Eilat to Metulla, students will enjoy nature, hikes, beaches, as well as political, historical, and archaeological sites. Tiyulim provide a well-earned break from the rigors of the Beit Midrash, and a chance to recharge ourselves for continued growth in our learning.
- **Any other activities or accommodations included in cost:** Please reach out for more details
- **Additional add on (that can affect cost):** Does not include medical insurance or laundry services. Please reach out for more details

Religious Observance and/or Program Philosophy:

Orthodox. The yeshiva expects each student to be fully committed to Shmirat HaMitzvot.

MIGDAL HaTORAH

(Continued)

Program Highlights:

- A short walk from the Yeshiva are both tennis courts and an indoor pool.
- Families in the community are always hosting students for Shabbat.

OHR DAVID

• info@ohrdavid.org • (02) 563-2826 • (02) 563-2846

Description of Program:

Ohr David is about honing in our students' strengths, and helping them flourish to the best person they can be.

Ohr David's unique approach to yeshiva, Torah, and jewish living empowers our young men to expand their knowledge build, and achieve their goals. Our staff is carefully recruited to bring these goals to life, to have the bigger picture, and provide the guidance so our students thrive.

Length of Program:

September to June

Location of Program:

Harav Chizkiya Shabtai 8, Jerusalem, Israel

Supervision:

At Ohr David, we encourage our students to be a part and contribute to the ongoing legacy of Torah, by bringing their own unique character, personality and perspectives to each sugya.

We invest in our students to learn, but to develop tools to teach Torah. We encourage our students to give shiurim in the Yeshiva to further their skills.

Cost Range:

Please contact for more details.

- **What are living arrangements like:** Please contact for more details
- **# of Meals:** Please contact for more details

- **Trips:** Please contact for more details
- **Any other activities or accommodations included in cost:** Please contact for more details
- **Additional add on (that can affect cost):** Please contact for more details

Religious Observance and/or Program Philosophy:

Orthodox

Program Highlights:

- Many guest speakers come speak at Ohr David
- Many amazing trips

SHA'AREI MEVASERET ZION

www.ysmz.org
Rav Shimon Isaacson • office@ysmz.org.il
Phone: 972-2-533-9100 or (347) 464-6513 • Fax: 972-2-533-9101

Description of Program:

Yeshivat Sha'arei Mevaseret Zion seeks to nurture students into well-rounded, leadership-oriented Bnei Torah with the following core attributes: a love of learning, a commitment to excel in both *mitzvot bein adam l'makom* and *bein adam l'chaveiro*, a love and appreciation of all Jews, a deep-felt connection to Eretz Yisrael, and a commitment to Yahadut.

We seek to promote these qualities in our Talmidim by drawing from the wellsprings of all perspectives within the Torah spectrum and by addressing the unique needs of each individual Talmid. We strive to create an energized and fun atmosphere in which each Talmid feels positive about his Judaism, his religious development, his friends, and his yeshiva.

Length of Program:

September to June

Location of Program:

Mevaseret Zion (outskirts of Jerusalem)

Supervision:

Religious Observance Required: Full commitment to Shmirat Torah U'mitzvot is a prerequisite.

Cost Range:

$28,900 USD; this includes registration, and below.

- **What are living arrangements like:** dormitory facilities

- **# of Meals:** Three meals a day
- **Trips:** Please contact for more details
- **Any other activities or accommodations included in cost:** Tiyulim, all Shabbatot and Chagim. Please contact for more details
- **Additional add on (that can affect cost):** Please contact for more details

Religious Observance and/or Program Philosophy:

Orthodox

Program Highlights:

- There is a weight room on campus and an outdoor basketball court. Indoor basketball court can be rented twice a week. There is also a running chug with one of the senior rabbanim.
- The yeshiva views the tiyulim as an integral part of the educational programming. There are five major overnight trips and at least one day trip per month. These are designed to enhance knowledge and love of Eretz Yisrael and jewish history, both ancient and modern.
- We also promote a weekly chesed program on Tuesday afternoons whereby the yeshiva participates in Shalva and other organizations, depending on the schedule. Chesed programs over the years have included volunteering for Magen David Adom, Hadassah Children's Hospital, Kedma, table-to-table, Yad Eliezer, Meir Panim Soup Kitchens, Amutat Efrat, babysitting for Kollel members and tutoring Ethiopian *olim* in Mevaseret Zion.

SHA'AREI MEVASERET ZION

(Continued)

Student Highlights:

- "The most unique thing about Mevaseret, that stood out to me, and made my year there as spectacular as it was, is the diversity of educators that Mevaseret offers. Each Rabbi has his own hashkafa (philosophy towards life) and comes from a different walk of life, which provides the student with a broadened perspective into Judaism."

- "Mevaseret looks for down-to-earth guys that want to grow. Everyone in Mevaseret is friendly and easy to get along with."

- "Location. Every yeshiva and seminary has their locational perks. Mevaseret is located right outside Jerusalem and is only a fifteen-minute bus to town. This provides the best atmosphere to be able to focus being outside the busy city, yet when you need to go to the city it is just a short bus ride away."

TIFERET YERUSHALAYIM

www.tiferet.org.il
Rabbi Chananya Greenwald • office@tiferet.org.il
Phone: (02) 643-7860 • Fax: (02) 644-6553

Description of Program:

To help students form a relationship with Hashem and the Torah that will instruct their actions and lives. To help students recognize their strengths, abilities, and place in the world so they can live productive, Jewish, self-aware, reflective lives. To help them pursue, attain, disseminate, and apply the wisdom of the Torah throughout their lives in the personal, communal, and professional spheres. Level of learning offered is intermediate to advanced—familiarity with Aramaic and Talmudic terminology and concepts is necessary. Must have an intermediate level of Hebrew—shiurim are in English but are liberally sprinkled with Hebrew phrases and terms.

Length of Program:

September to June

Location of Program:

24/5 Hakablan Jerusalem

Supervision:

Please contact for more details

Cost Range:

Tuition: $21,000 includes dormitory, meals, instruction, and tiyulim

- **What are living arrangements like:** Dormitory
- **# of Meals:** Please contact for more details
- **Trips:** Please contact for more details

- **Any other activities or accommodations included in cost?:** Please contact for more details
- **Additional add on (that can affect cost):** Please contact for more details

Religious Observance and/or Program Philosophy:

Orthodox; participants must have a ommitment to Torah and mitzvos.

Program Highlights:

- *Special Informal Programs:* Guest speakers, extra learning incentive programs, Melavei Malka, Rosh Chodesh seudot.
- *Interaction with Israelis:* An average of one tiyul per month. Students are not encouraged to be involved politically in Israel but there are ample opportunities for interaction with the hundreds of Israelis on campus.
- *Sports Facilities:* There is a weight room, ping-pong room, indoor basketball court (gym), music room and outdoor basketball courts.

TORAH TECH (MENS)

TorahTech.co
Info@TorahTech.co • +1914-336-4313

Description of Program:

Torah Tech is a unique gap-year program in Israel for young adults that integrates intensive Torah study with professional development through business and tech internships. Our multifaceted program challenges students to strive for excellence both religiously and professionally, by immersing them in the world of Torah and ruchniyut, as well as the world of high-powered Israeli businesses and tech companies. This rare combination can only be found in Eretz Yisrael, the eternal homeland of Am Yisrael and the birthplace of unparalleled innovation and advancement in business and technology.

Students will also connect to the land of Israel through exciting trips and tours, give back to the community through chesed projects and volunteer work, hear from distinguished religious personalities from both the Torah and corporate worlds, and enjoy exclusive access to nearby gyms, men-only beaches, self defense training courses, and much more. The result? Students who will have developed into passionate, independent, and empowered young adults with the necessary tools to succeed as bnei Torah in the modern world. At Torah Tech, you won't just learn Torah, you'll live it.

Length of Program:

9 months

Location of Program:

Ranana

Supervision:

Our post-high school Gap Year program is meant for mature, responsible, and passionate young men who genuinely seek to deepen their connection to God, Israel, and the Jewish people through intensive Torah study and authentic, real-life modern Israel. Students should be both highly motivated to, as well as capable of, living independently, growing religiously, and succeed both academically and in a workplace environment.
Visit our website for staff information.

Cost Range:

Please contact for more details.

- **What are living arrangements like:** Torah Tech Mens is located in Tel Aviv, the heart of central Israel and the home of start-up nation. Students will live in several apartments inside the city, each equipped with a kitchen, several full bathrooms, and living areas. Daily Torah study will take place in a centrally located Beit Midrash. Students will enjoy easy access to public transportation, close proximity to gyms, synagogues, beaches, museums, and malls, and the unique opportunity to experience life in modern Israel first-hand.
- **# of Meals:** Three meals a day
- **Trips:** See all of ancient and modern Israel. From hikes through caves to conferences featuring top Israeli investors, you'll connect to the past, present, and future of our homeland and our people.
- **Any other activities or accommodations included in cost:** With options for gym membership, krav maga army training, biking, surfing, volleyball, basketball, baseball, our students are constantly

active. Men's only beaches offer the perfect setting for down time as well.

- **Additional add on (that can affect cost):** Please contact for more details

Religious Observance and/or Program Philosophy:

Orthodox: We aim to deliver knowledge, tools, and once-in-a-lifetime experiences to our students so they can discover their religious identity and purpose, build their professional future, and be fully prepared to succeed in the next stages of life.

Program Highlights:

- Learning from professionals
- Personal attention
- High level internships

Student Highlights:

"Torah Tech is the perfect Gap Year program for someone who wants to experience Israel through both a spiritual and professional lens. Yehuda and Rabbi have created an environment in which guys can see what it's like to be a religious Jew in the real world. Torah Tech is a no compromise program—you will get time to learn, time to work, time to chill, time to bond, time to eat (the food is incredible) and time to grow. My experience at Torah Tech is irreplaceable and I have made lifelong friends and connections."
      —Gabriel

"Torah Tech is an incredible Gap Year experience that allowed me to explore my personal, academic, professional, and religious interests and grow in every aspect. The administration is made up of an incredible group of people who can and will act as lifelong mentors who I have confided in when I had any issues during my year in Israel and beyond. My internship in cancer immunotherapy research at one of the premier hospitals in Israel was absolutely fantastic and provided a fascinating glimpse into the world of Israeli biotechnology. I was also surrounded by an amazing group of peers who were doing incredible work in a variety of high-tech fields and influenced my academic interests greatly. Besides those influences, I consider the Torah Tech squad among my closest friends and I will be forever grateful to the program for bringing us together. On a separate note, the tech conferences and trips that Torah Tech planned gave me a deep appreciation for both Israel's rich past as a cultural/religious homeland for the Jewish people as well as its exciting future as the Startup Nation whose lands flow with high-tech innovations. Lastly, the Jewish learning that the program provides is one of a kind with a unique blend of philosophy and text to create an experience par excellence.

"All in all, there is not a single experience I can endorse more highly than a Gap Year at Torah Tech. My Gap Year was the most formative year of my life and I have only Torah Tech to thank."

—Daniel

"I came to Torah Tech with one goal in mind: to strengthen my Jewish identity while setting up my future career. I can definitely say that Torah Tech is helping me accomplish this goal and more.

"Yehuda, the Program Director, goes above and beyond in everything we do from the amazing food, beautiful living conditions, setting us up with amazing internships, and just straight up being one of the nicest people I've ever met. The program's rabbinical leader, Rav Shlomo Chen, is the greatest rabbi that I have ever had. His shiurim are thoughtful, inspiring, and always encourage me to do my best. Every shiur this year has challenged me to think in ways that I never had before about topics that I had previously dismissed as mundane.

"The internships that they entrusted their eighteen-year-old students with are insane. Every student is interested in real jobs, with real responsibilities. Most students work in a startup environment, so every hand counts. We are really treated as full members of the companies we work in, and there's never a dull moment. The internship content spans across high-tech, medicine, photography—really anything your heart desires—Yehuda and Rav Shlomo are well connected enough to get an internship for you in any field you want. Personally, I work as a programmer in a high-tech startup and my work is being used by my company daily. I am thankful to Torah Tech for the wonderful Gap Year they gave me the opportunity for.

"Everyone at Torah Tech knows that they only get out as much as they put in. The dynamics of the program are run like the startups we work in. We're a small, personal team where if you aren't positively affecting your peers then you aren't doing enough. When just one of us is late for davening or shiur, or doesn't clean up his fair share of the apartment, all of us feel the repercussions.

"You get what you give: if you let this program mean the world to you, you will receive the world in return."

—Gregory

TORAT SHRAGA

www.toratshraga.com • office@toratshraga.com
(02) 642-9907

Description of Program:

To guide its students in developing self-proficiency in the examination of Talmudic and Torah texts. This is achieved through methodological techniques of rigorous conceptual analysis while simultaneously providing them the opportunity to acquire a vast knowledge utilizing the bekiut incentive program. To nurture and foster a close rebbe/talmud relationship and provide them with spiritual and intellectual role models that will anchor them Jewishly and emotionally.

To broaden their knowledge and connectedness to Eretz Yisrael and Medinat Yisrael via tiyulim and shabbatonim and a welfare of experiential encounters that will arouse and deepen their spiritual roots. This is accomplished in sync with their deepening commitment to observance of mitzvot and the strengthening of the tenets of our faith.

Length of Program:

September to June

Location of Program:

Bait Vegan, Jerusalem

Supervision:

The behavior of the students is closely monitored by the faculty. Although there is no curfew, students must spend the night in the dormitory unless he was granted permission to do otherwise. No smoking is permitted in the yeshiva and there is a zero tolerance policy regarding alcohol and drugs.

TORAT SHRAGA

(Continued)

Cost Range:

$27,000, which includes room, board, and tiyulim.

- **What are living arrangements like:** Four person and two person rooms are offered. Four person rooms come with a bathroom and a small kitchen area.

  - *Living Quarters:* YTS rents dormitory space on campus from YU. There are two to four in newly renovated dorm rooms. Each room has its own bathroom and kitchenette. The students get to choose their own roommates prior to their arrival. Once every three shabbatot or so, students are permitted to entertain guests.
  - *Availability of Private Kitchen Facilities:* Each room has its own kitchenette with refrigerator.
  - *Facility use during Shabbat and Yom Tov:* The yeshiva is open every Shabbat and Yom Tov from the day the students arrive till they leave. Often members of the Gruss Kollel provide home-hospitality on Shabbat and Yom Tov.
- **# of Meals:** Please reach out for more details
- **Trips:** YTS has three three-day tiyulim along with regular smaller one-day tiyulim throughout the year.
- **Any other activities or accommodations included in cost:** Please reach out for more details
- **Additional add on (that can affect cost):** Please reach out for more details

Religious Observance and/or Program Philosophy:

Orthodox

TORAT SHRAGA

(Continued)

Program Highlights:

- Every Sunday there is an Halacha shiur given by the Rosh HaYeshiva to the entire yeshiva. Rabbi David's vast experience as both Community Rabbi and Rosh Yeshiva creates a rare blend of practical halacha and thorough analyses of the methodology of the halachic decisors. For many, the highlight of their week is Rav David's Halacha shiur which is in the form of an open forum for all halachic and/or hashkafic queries.
- The latter part of the Afternoon Seder is focused on subject matter other than Gemara. Twice a week, in the six to seven p.m. slot, the Rosh HaYeshiva says a shiur or a sicha in Chumash and contemporary issues. Rav Olshin runs a popular seminar called "Kiruv Training Seminar." Based on the mishna in Pirkei Avot, every Jew should be equipped with the tools and information needed to present the beauty and philosophy of Torah Judaism to others less schooled in these areas. This class aims to arm the students with the fundamentals of our faith in a clear and cogent manner so that it may be shared and conveyed with the larger community.
- On Monday Nights, Rab Yaakov Haber renowned author and lecturer gives a shiur on the topic of Tefilah. Afterward, all students participate in a vaad/bayit cham at the homes of the Gruss Kollel.

Student Highlights:

- We are on the YU Israel campus.
- It's very easy to form a strong bond with your rabbis.
- The atmosphere around the building is always electric.

YESHIVAT ASHREINU

www.ashreinu.org.il
Rabbi Gotch Yudin • info@ashreinu.org.il • +972-54-219-4982
(Israel cell and WhatsApp) • 201-338-5150 (American number
that goes straight to his Israel cell)

Description of Program:

Yeshivat Ashreinu is an innovative yeshiva that instills a lifelong love and commitment to Torah, Am Yisrael, and Eretz Yisrael in our students. We accomplish this through our unique curriculum that combines dynamic Torah study, meaningful Chesed internships, and challenging Tiyulim. Ashreinu features a warm and caring environment where our energetic, knowledgeable, and relatable staff is dedicated to the development and growth of each and every student.

Length of Program:

9.5 months. Late August to mid-June

Location of Program:

Beit Shemesh

Supervision:

Our students live in a spacious campus with state-of-the-art facilities. Our dorms are overseen by our warm and caring Av and Eim Bayit as well as madrichim.

Cost Range:

$27,200; scholarships are available for qualified students.

- **What are living arrangements like:** Room and board in our dorms is included

- **# of Meals:** Three meals a day
- **Trips:** Weekly trips
- **Any other activities or accommodations included in cost?:** Chesed opportunities and everything in between are all included. Please call for more details.
- **Additional add on (that can affect cost):** Please call for more details.

Religious Observance and/or Program Philosophy:

Ashreinu is a Modern Orthodox Zionistic Yeshiva.

Program Highlights:

- *Weekly tiyulim!* Our weekly tiyulim are an integral part of our yeshiva. There is no better way to appreciate the beauty of Israel—while expanding your knowledge of jewish history—than by hiking, riding, climbing, and swimming across the country. We transfer our Land—from the deserts of the South to the mountains in the North—into our classroom. At Ashreinu, we don't just learn about our heritage, we live it.
- *Meaningful chesed internships!* At Ashreinu, we put our learning into practice. In addition to a weekly group chesed trip, students design their bi-weekly individual chesed internships based on their personal interests and talents. Through this empowering experience, students have the opportunity to develop themselves, give back to others, and to create a Kiddush Hashem.
- *Dynamic torah study!* Ashreinu's Torah study curriculum is well rounded and designed to immerse students in the areas of Torah most relevant to their daily lives. Students are encouraged to

challenge, probe, and question. Our Rebbeim help nurture a life of Torah in our students, while giving them a deeper understanding of our religion. With an average of six students per class, our students receive individual guidance from a diverse staff of Rebbeim.

Student Highlights:

"Attending Ashreinu was one of the most influential experiences of my life. I have vivid memories of all my rabbeim and their respective shiurim. The unforgettable volunteer experiences at Shalva doing water therapy with children with special needs and teaching martial arts to local Israeli students. And of course, the friendships made throughout the year. Rabbi Yudin gave me the chance to learn hilchos shabbos from a book series by helping me pay for them. I learned from them each day for the rest of the year and regularly reference them today. Thank you for supporting my learning and growth from day one of Ashreinu through today."

 —Nadav

"Before Ashreinu, as a Jew, I felt small. A small part of a small nation. How can I be a light unto the world? How can I be a Jew in the modern world? How can I have my cake and eat it too? Rabbi Gotch Yudin and the rest of the Ashreinu Rebbeim not only answered these questions for me, but inspired me to live my life as a proud Jew, husband, and father in the Holy Land."

 —Eli

"I went to Ashreinu on a whim, with little attachment to Israel and an amateur understanding of the value of a Gap Year. Somehow, Ashreinu managed to connect me to the Land, kickstart my Torah learning, take me on the best adventures of my life, throw me into the high-octane life

YESHIVAT ASHREINU

(Continued)

---

of volunteering for Magen David Adom, and cultivate some of the best relationships I have. Even if I had gone in with high expectations, Ashreinu would have surpassed them."

—Jesse

YESHIVAT ERETZ HATZVI

www.yehatzvi.org

Description of Program:

Yeshivat Eretz HaTzvi is a proudly Zionist post-high school program whose goal is to engage our students in a love of and commitment to Torah study and observance as well as to the land of Israel. Our excellent faculty inspires our students in a wide variety of subjects that include not only Talmud and Tanach (Bible) but also engage them in Jewish history, law (Halacha), philosophy and the study of prayer, customs, and tradition.

Now located on the Jerusalem College of Technology campus, we will share a Beit Midrash with religious Israeli students as well as enjoying a beautiful campus with state-of-the-art fitness rooms and sports facilities. Our goal is for students to become informed, proud, and dynamic leaders in college and ultimately in their careers and their communities. Men's post-high school (Shana Aleph and Bet).

Length of Program:

Approximately 10 months

Location of Program:

Jerusalem College of Technology Campus, Givat Mordechai neighborhood in Jerusalem

Supervision:

Beside the full administrative and academic faculty, there are an Av and Eim Bayit in charge of the dormitory and there are several madrichim (counselors) who live in the dormitory full time. Usually one madrich for every twelve to fifteen students.

Cost Range:

$27,500

Full week of classes and lectures; room and full board; tiyulim (trips) including entry fees and transportation; WiFi/internet access.

- **What are living arrangements like:** Dormitory. Two students per room and each room with its own bathroom.
- **# of Meals:** Three meals per day
- **Trips:** At least one trip every three weeks
- **Any other activities or accommodations included in cost:** Three days in Eilat; several shabbatonim; three-day Yam l'Yam tiyul
- **Additional add on (that can affect cost):** Approximately ten annual "yemei iyun" (panel discussions and in-depth studies) of vital topics such as Judaism and the role of women, Jewish sexual ethics; Torah and the secular world (art, science, literature); non-Jews and Halacha. Presented by experts in each field. (No extra cost)

Religious Observance and/or Program Philosophy:

We are a modern, centrist Orthodox school with full observance of Halacha, Kashrut, and Shabbat.

Program Highlights:

- Broad Torah curriculum from Gemara to philosophy and Tanach to Jewish History taught by expert, dynamic, and approachable teachers.
- Design your own learning schedule—choose from options throughout the day and find your passion in Torah.

- International student body including groups from Australia, South Africa, Europe, and England.

Student Highlights:

"Tanach at Eretz HaTzvi isn't just Chumash with Rashi. It's engaging with Tanach experts to really understand the stories, messages, and lessons of the text."

    —Elisha

"I came to Eretz HaTzvi to experience more than just Gemara. At Eretz HaTzvi the combinations of classes are limitless."

    —Akiva

"The opportunity to pursue Machshava daily is unique to Eretz HaTzvi."

    —Sam

YESHIVAT LEV HaTORAH

www.levhatorah.org • R Michael Cytrin
mcytrin@levhatorah.org • +972 50 522 8280

Description of Program:

Yeshivat Lev HaTorah is a full-time Torah learning program. Our mission is to nurture inspired, confident, well-rounded bnei Torah with the skills to learn independently, while simultaneously developing a deep devotion to Medinat Yisrael, and the entire Jewish community. We strive to tap into each of our student's individual strengths to help them understand how they have a unique and individualized relationship with our G-d and our community.

Length of Program:

10 months

Location of Program:

Ramat Shilo, Beit Shemesh

Supervision:

Lev HaTorah is proud to provide a large staff to allow students to achieve their educational and personal goals. There is a counselor that focuses on religious growth as well as a full-time mental health professional.

Cost Range:

All formal and informal educational programs, room and board are included in the price. Flight, health insurance, and phone plan are not included in the price.

- **What are living arrangements like:** The dorm building is made up of nine apartments. Each apartment houses on average twelve boys and is equipped with a kitchen and a laundry space. Most apartments feature a balcony which allows for great views of the Beit Shemesh scenery.

- **# of Meals:** Three delicious meals daily every day from day one; you are in Israel until the day you leave.
- **Trips:** Trips are spread out throughout the year and are set up to inspire a love for the Land of Israel. There are longer trips where we sleep off campus and pack the day with fun and exciting activities. There are also day trips to visit in-person the places that the stories of the Tanach happened as well as to get a much needed respite from the learning routine.
- **Any other activities or accommodations included in cost:** Please reach out for more details
- **Additional add on:** The yeshiva offers an optional yet incredibly inspiring week-long trip to Poland. There are optional weekly activities in mountain biking and Krav Maga self-defense.

Religious Observance and/or Program Philosophy:

We are a Religious Zionist Modern Orthodox Institution and the expectation is of our students to be religiously observant by keeping Shabbat and following the orthodox dietary code as well as the rest of the halacha's instruction.

Program Highlights:

- *Individual Attention:* a large and available staff of Rabbeim who live in the neighborhood of the yeshiva help you (a) build your unique place in Judaism in a warm atmosphere and (b) discover strengths and insights you never knew you were capable of revealing.

YESHIVAT LEV HaTORAH

(Continued)

- *Exciting informal program*: to sweeten the experience of learning and living in Israel. Expand your horizons outside the text to be a well-rounded Jew!
- *Your home away from home*: the bed you receive on day one is your bed the entire year. You are never kicked out. Food is cooked fresh three meals a day. This is your home!

Student Highlights:

"Lev HaTorah is full of guys who are generally laid-back and easy to work with, and since Lev HaTorah is located in Ramat Beit Shemesh, it's easier to feel part of a community and part of a neighborhood. Also, while the trips are fun, there are some spiritual, educational, and historical aspects of the trips."

—Oren (AIGYA Ambassador)

"Lev Haotrah is great because of the wide variety of Shiur selection. The large staff of lev Haotrah allows for everyone to find someone to connect to."

—Michael

"Lev offers students a chance to incorporate a strong Jewish community around them, with a learning environment that fits them. This combination allows everyone to feel comfortable as they grow and merit as Jews and as people."

—Netanel

YESHIVAT NETIV ARYEH

Natan Schwartz • schwartz.natan@gmail.com

Description of Program:
In the heart of the Jewish Quarter of Jerusalem's Old City, opposite the Kotel HaMaaravi, we focus on love of G-d, Torah, the Jewish people, and the Land of Israel. Daily interaction, shiurim, and chugim with the yeshiva's Rabbanim, Educational Staff and Israeli Kollel are a key component in solidifying these core values. Our large and diverse staff under the leadership of Rav Aharon Bina gives the warmth and personal attention needed to help our students mature and become the best they can be, not only as Jews, but as human beings.

Length of Program:

10 months

Location of Program:

Kotel Plaza, Old City of Jerusalem

Supervision:

Madrichim living with and guiding the students all of the time, and full-time security personnel.

Cost Range:

$28,000 for full room and board, including all shabbatot and vacation times, trips, health insurance.

- **What are living arrangements like:** Recently renovated dormitory a few minutes walk from the Yeshiva, American mattresses, workout room, heating and cooling.
- **# of Meals:** All, including all Shabbatot and holidays.

YESHIVAT NETIV ARYEH

(Continued)

- **Trips:** Throughout the year. Monthly day trips, plus three 3-day trips. Trips are a very important component of our program on various levels. First, it's important for us to see and appreciate the land of Israel. In addition, trips are used to help bond the students with the students and students with the staff. Lastly, it helps give a break from a pretty rigorous schedule. We want to teach our students to be dedicated and devoted to their schedules but at the same time know how to be balanced, take breaks, and enjoy the world around them.
- **Any other activities or accommodations included in cost:** Please reach out for more details
- **Additional add on (that can affect cost):** Please reach out for more details

Religious Observance and/or Program Philosophy:

Orthodox—Zionist

Program Highlights:

- Shiurim for every academic level, Ulpon Hebrew classes, and classes on a wide range of topics.
- Large hands on caring staff!
- Location! In the Kotel Plaza, with a large balcony overlooking the Western Wall.

Student Highlights:

- "The best part about being in Netiv is the family feeling that I felt both during my time in yeshiva and even more when I left."

- "Having the opportunity to learn one-on- one with a rabbi at night seder is something that will last with me forever."
- "The time spent in the dorms with the other guys. I made friend-ships and relationships with guys from all over the United States and England that will last forever. Not to mention the extremely dedicated staff that left an unforgettable impact on me that will last a lifetime."

YESHIVAT ORAYTA

www.orayta.org • Office@orayta.org

Description of Program:

Yeshivat Orayta is a broad-thinking, text based yeshiva study program for motivated post-high school students. Our carefully selected student body is intellectually open, spiritually curious and passionate about Jewish learning and personal growth. Our daily schedule consists of a blend of classical Talmud study combined with a diverse set of classes and conversations in Jewish philosophy, Jewish law, and Biblical studies. At Yeshivat Orayta, students gain the skills to study independently as well as a rich background and understanding of the meaning behind Jewish life and practice.

Length of Program:

Late August until early June

Location of Program:

Old City of Jerusalem

Supervision:

Multiple dorm counselors, plus two full-time program counselors.

Cost Range:

$28,000 (scholarship available)

- **What are living arrangements like:** Dormitory living, three to four students per room
- **# of Meals:** Three daily
- **Trips:** One to two days a month
- **Any other activities or accommodations included in cost:** Please reach out for more details

- **Additional add on (that can affect cost):** Poland trip—additional cost

Religious Observance and/or Program Philosophy:

Modern Orthodox

Program Highlights:

- Focus on both the "what" as well as the "why" of Judaism (text-based learning together with philosophical emphasis of meaning).
- Small classes with low student–teacher ratio.
- Intellectually and spiritually diverse staff combined with geographically diverse student body.

Student Highlights:

- "... Orayta and how it's shaped my interaction with education and the quest for knowledge. Orayta does not shy away from questions. In fact, the Rebbeim encourage it. They understand that everyone there has questions about G-d, our religion, our practices, or even about the world as a whole and its general philosophies and ideologies. The Rebbeim give us the tools, habits, and goals to live a successful Jewish life. They understand that for that goal to become a reality we can't have just the *how* and *what* of Judaism without the *why*. We need to understand why we do what we do, what deeper meaning there is behind the seemingly mundane, and how to grapple with our crises of faith . . . If a Rav or a student makes a point that troubles you, you don't keep it to yourself but you challenge. You probe deeper until you find the truth you were seeking. Students are constantly respectfully challenging each other

on assumed truths until they both walk away feeling like they've come to a deeper understanding . . . the Beit Midrash has an air of love, camaraderie, and a pursuit of intellectual and even emotional understandings . . . I've gained incredible mentors and an understanding of what a mentor even is. Orayta gave me Rebbeim who are always open to talking on the phone and answering questions, whether Torah related or just general. They will always be there to guide me and every other student through personal struggles . . . the end of the Orayta year does not at all mean the end of our ongoing student Rebbe relationships."

- ". . . the atmosphere of intellectual honesty, the rich spirituality embodied by so many of the staff members and students, and the lead-by-example model personified by our Rabbis, come together to make Orayta what it is, an incredible institution uniquely positioned to guide students toward a completely novel way of viewing Torah. It's not just a topic to study, it's a lens through which to view the totality of life, something that begs to be experienced rather than simply explained."

- "I was able to truly understand what it means to take ownership over my Jewish identity . . . It was amazing to see how everyone in Yeshiva was finding their unique project; everyone was taking ownership over their learning in their own way."

YESHIVAT SHA'ALVIM

http://www.shaalvim.org/yeshiva/
office@usshaalvim.org • (718) 677-7200

Description of Program:

Yeshivat Sha'alvim is a hesder yeshiva emphasizing Torah study and observance as integral components of Jewish life. It is known for its strong *Beit Midrash* and high-level *shiurim*, focusing specifically on teaching conceptual methodology.

Spirited *tishes* and *ruach* are a central part of the experience. With a strong religious Zionist character, Sha'alvim seeks to instill a deep appreciation for Israel. Nestled in the beautiful Ayalon Valley, halfway between Jerusalem and Tel Aviv and removed from the distractions of a busy city, students immerse themselves in their development as *Bnei Torah*. As a hesder yeshiva, international students can choose to combine intensive Torah study with active service in the IDF. The yeshiva greatly stresses individualism, providing an inviting atmosphere and personal attention to allow each student to find his own *derech* in *avodat Hashem*. Almost all the Rabbanim live on campus, welcoming students into their homes forging life-long relationships.

Length of Program:

10 months

Location of Program:

Sha'alvim

Supervision:

There is a program counselor, yet at the same time relative independence for students with responsibilities is expected.

YESHIVAT SHA'ALVIM

(Continued)

Cost Range:

Shana Aleph (first year)—$27,500
Shana Bet (second year)—$22,000
All included—classes, room, board, trips

- **What are living arrangements like:** Dorm
- **# of Meals:** Three
- **Trips:** Monthly Tiyulim/Shabbatons, optional Friday trips
- **Any other activities or accommodations included in cost:** N/A
- **Additional add on (that can affect cost):** N/A

Religious Observance and/or Program Philosophy:

Modern Orthodox Hesder

Program Highlights:

- High-level, rigorous daily learning.
- Respect for individual growth promoted by positive energy and guidance.
- Far enough from Jerusalem to facilitate focused studies, but close enough to enjoy the experience.

Student Highlights:

From AIGYA Ambassador Yoni Bean:

- "Incredible independence and a wide range of role models and outlooks to learn from."
- "An energetic, motivated learning environment surrounding one with like-minded individuals."
- "A beautiful campus integrated and insulated in a warm community outside of Jerusalem."

YESHIVAT TORAH V'AVODAH (YTVA)

ytvaisrael.org
office@tvaisrael.org • Israel: 0507098304
US line in Israel: 646-248-7555 • US office: 212-465-9536

Description of Program:

Yeshivat Torah v'Avodah is an elite and innovative Bnei Akiva yeshiva for highly motivated high school graduates. In one incredible year, you will experience life-changing growth in your connection to Torah, to the Jewish people, and to the Land and State of Israel. You will have the opportunity to learn at the highest level in Eretz Chemdah, the most elite and impressive Religious Zionist Torah institution in the world, where you will form deep and long-lasting connections with the future leaders of Am Yisrael. Because we believe that learning in Israel must extend outside the four walls of the beit-midrash, we embark on amazing tiyulim and other only in Israel experiences that will give you a keen love for, and appreciation of, our land and its people.

Length of Program:

10 months

Location of Program:

Katamon, Jerusalem

Supervision:

An Av and Eym-Bayit live in the dormitory building, as do several madrichim. Most of the Rabbanim and other staff members live nearby and are extremely hands-on. Everyone is expected to interact with students, staff, society, and Hashem with the highest degree of respect at all times.

242

YESHIVAT TORAH V'AVODAH (YTVA)

(Continued)

Cost Range:

$29,500

- **What are living arrangements like:** Dorm
- **# of Meals:** Three daily
- **Trips:** Many—Shabbatonim, Eilat trip, other overnight trips, some day-trips, one week on a religious kibbutz, Poland journey
- **Any other activities or accommodations included in cost:** All trips included in cost, except Poland
- **Additional add on (that can affect cost):** Medical insurance is not included in the cost

Religious Observance and/or Program Philosophy:

Religious Zionist

Program Highlights:

- Unbelievably caring, devoted, and charismatic staff.
- Innovative approach to Torah learning which fosters lifelong love of Torah and preparation for life as a Torah-observant Jew after the year in Israel.
- Engagement with Eretz Yisrael, Am Yisrael, and Torat Yisrael.

Student Highlights:

- "One of the many memorable trips we had this year was when we traveled to a Kibbutz Ein HaNatziv for a week. It was the highlight of my year because we had the opportunity to work the land, eat the amazing homegrown food, relax at the natural spring, interact

---

with the amazing Israeli culture and have some of the most memorable nights of the year."

- "The popular Vatikin Rosh Chodesh minyanim lead by our Rosh Yeshiva, Rav Yair, is something not to be missed. It takes place at the Kotel early in the morning. Every single time it is jam packed with high energy, intense dancing, powerful singing, and pure joy as we pull in everyone we can from the sidelines to come join us."

- "The morning shiurs we were in didn't always stay in the beis. Some of the most memorable times from this year were when our morning shiurs went the park to learn, and to the times we went to our Rav's house for breakfast at least once a month and learned Halacha and Gemara while we munched down on some great food we all made for each other."

YESHIVAT YISHREI LEV

www.yishrei.org
Rabbi Moshe Gordon • office@yishrei.org
(02) 579-5985/718-506-0147 • Fax: 057-796-1198
Rechov HaGr"a 8, P.O.B. 697 Kiryat Yearim

Description of Program:

Yishrei Lev strives to imbue its students with a desire for greatness in all that they do. Students should emerge from their stay in the Yeshiva with the skills and methodology for excellence in learning, both in depth and in broad knowledge. Students will learn and experience the thrill of personal growth and achievement in areas of character, interpersonal relationships, and religious observance. The Yeshiva aims to impart to its students a feeling of being part of the tradition of the classical Yeshivot and the ability to apply that tradition to their lives in the modern world. We offer an advanced level of learning—able to independently study Gemara texts. An intermediate knowledge of Hebrew is required.

Length of Program:

September to June

Location of Program:

Rechov HaGr"a 8

Supervision:

Please contact for more details.

Cost Range:

$24,500. Tuition includes room, board, tiyulim, and all academic activities.

- **What are living arrangements like:** Please reach out for more details

- **# of Meals:** Please reach out for more details
- **Trips:** Please reach out for more details
- **Any other activities or accommodations included in cost:** Please reach out for more details
- **Additional add on (that can affect cost):** Please reach out for more details

Religious Observance and/or Program Philosophy:

Orthodox; Yishrei Lev only accepts students with a full commitment to Shmirat Torah U'mitzvot.

Program Highlights:

- There are guest speakers for Chagigot and Yemei Iyun, Shabbatot, Melave Malka, etc. Music and Ruach are an important part of the Yishrei Lev experience.
- There are periodic tiyulim, including overnights.
- There are frequent Ruach filled In-Shabbatot that add to the dynamic feel of the Yeshiva. There are a number of off campus Shabbatonim in various communities that enable the students to experience different segments of Israeli society.

CHAPTER FIVE

AIGYA Ambassador
Fun Facts

The AIGYA Ambassadors are Gap Year Students from a variety of programs, specially selected by AIGYA to chronicle their Gap Year in real time on AIGYA's Instagram @israelgapyear. We hope their experiences and insights are helpful to you! Their quotes and photos are sprinkled throughout the book.

The Ambassadors have compiled a list of some fun facts about Israel and things that you might benefit from when preparing to go, or to use to make the most out of your year.

Thanks to all of our Ambassadors for making their Gap Year come alive for all of us. Big shout out to inaugural Lead Ambassadors Avi Proctor and Sarah Pape.

AIGYA AMBASSADORS

Talia Abel	*Israel Experience at Bar Ilan*
Gila Allen	*MMY*
Akiva Aryeh	*Hakotel*
Jeremy Asheghian	*Reishit*
Dina Bash	*Midreshet Lindenbaum*

Yoni Bean	*Sha'alvim for Boys*
Ariella Benaim	*Sha'alvim for Women*
Eliana Cohen	*Nativ*
Dylan Corn	*Aish Gesher*
AJ Eisenberg	*Yeshivat Torah V Avodah*
Matthew Ganchrow	*Nativ*
Aura Glazer	*Migdal Oz*
Gila Gordon	*Midreshet Moriah*
Ellie Jarashow	*Orayta*
Adira Kahn	*Baer Miriam*
Calev Knopf	*Kibbutz Ulpan Program*
Leorah Lalezari	*Tiferet*
Yali Miller	*Harova*
Rory Meyerson	*Sharie Mevaseret Zion*
Talia Paknoosh	*Midreshet Amit*
Sarah Pape	*Machon Maayan*
Avi Proctor	*Torat Shraga*
Mia Raskin	*Midreshet Torah V Avodah*
Oren Rimmon	*Lev HaTorah*
Eli Solomon	*Mayanot*
Orly Walker	*Midreshet Torat Chesed*
Lea Zarifpour	*Midreshet Tehillah*
Ellie Zisblatt	*Michalalah*

What Your Gap Year Program Does *Not* Tell You to Bring to Israel and Other Fun Facts

Packing tips: What to Bring

- Portable speaker—You will want to "chill"
- Portable charger—There are not a lot of outlets and everyone has some electronic device so this will come in handy

- Travel alarm clock—There are no wall clocks
- Watch—If you are Shabbat observant you will need this on Shabbat
- Shabbat lamp (travel lamp)—Also really convenient when roommate is sleeping and you want to read
- Sleeping bag liner—Keeps you safe
- Filtered water bottle—Water will never taste better on those hot middle eastern days
- Shower shoes—There are a lot of people using the shower
- Outlet extender—Don't get caught getting disconnected when a lot of people are around
- Space bag—Small spaces, makes for easier storage
- Laundry detergent-to-go stain remover—Quick fixer
- Heavy raincoat—It does rain in the winter so don't be caught in a downpour
- Laundry bag—Laundry services available, but you will still need these for efficiency
- Backpack—A must have for day trips and overnights
- Photos from home—Never underestimate the importance of something familiar

Tips: While in Israel

Groceries:

- Super Sol is the main supermarket that is all over Israel and they have a lot of American products.
- Makolet is like a corner store and they are all over Israel as well.

Bedding and Towels:

- Blanket Express. You can order any kind of bedding you need. It's in Israel and they can deliver straight to your program.

Water Heater:

- The water heater is not on continuously, so you have to turn on the water before you shower, but *beware:* once hot it is *very* hot. Test the temp before you jump in.

Getting around:

- Rav Kav is your metro card in Israel when you want to use the subway or bus. You can download the Rav Kav app to put more money on it or go to a station to add money to it.

Language:

- The main language is Hebrew. If your program has an Ulpan, you will be talking like a native in a few short weeks. But the second most-spoken language is English. So do not worry— you will have no trouble communicating.

Don't Leave Israel Without Doing or Seeing This

- Eilat: See the amazing city that is at the southern tip of Israel. They have great malls, beaches, and fun activities to do.
- Masada: Hike with your friends. The history of Masada is wild. It is so worth seeing.
- Negev: Tough mountains to hike but amazing views.
- Golan heights: You can go rafting and hiking and have a great time with your friends.

- Tzfat. A magical city with so much history.
- Dead Sea: Floating in the sea is a very cool experience.
- Tel Aviv: Very urban and fun but don't forget to visit the shuk and the beach at Sunset.
- Haifa: A fun city with a very diverse, young community.
- Bahai Gardens: Incredibly beautiful with amazing views of the sea.
- Benyamina: About forty km to the south of Haifa; beautiful area.
- Tachana Rishona: The first train station in Jerusalem.
- Chanukah: Go to the old city any night for an amazing atmosphere as everyone lights the menorah outside their houses.
- Purim: Spend it outside of Jerusalem and then the next day in Jerusalem. Israel is unique in that you can celebrate Purim for two straight days. It's a wild experience to take part in.
- The Israeli Holocaust museum, Yad Vashem: This is the most amazing Holocaust Museum in the world with so much history to learn. It's a very meaningful experience, especially because you are in Israel.
- Music: Go to a concert and explore Israeli music.

Take Advantage of Every Weekend to Experience Shabbat Around Israel

Top places to spend Shabbat & holidays

- Jerusalem. Anywhere in Jerusalem can provide a great Shabbat experience but a Shabbat in the old city is a must-do during your Gap Year experience
- Machlis Family for Friday night. Famous family in Jerusalem that hosts dinners. Ask your program to arrange.

- Going to Hebron for Parsha Chaya Sarah. It's one weekend every year where thousands of people are there for this holy time of year. You can sleep in a school nearby or in a tent. Ask your program about it.
- Safed. Highest city in Israel. A unique and artistic part of Israel where Jewish mysticism was born.
- Meron for Log B'omer.
- Kibbutz. Very relaxing and meditative Shabbat experience away from a city.
- Karmiel. North Israel small community with beautiful surrounding scenery.
- Teachers' homes. Students enjoy having Shabbos with their teachers from school and it's a comfortable setting.
- You can even check out other Gap Year programs over the weekend. Join a friend in another program as a guest to experience what their weekend is like.

Recommended Restaurants in Israel

- Tzidkiyahu
- Piccolino
- The Waffle Factory
- Cafe Rimon (desserts)
- Blondie
- Crave
- Roza
- Club Sushi Rehavia
- Luciana
- Pompidou
- Harvey's Steakhouse
- Burger Market

- Mr. Green
- Station 9
- Shosh Cafe
- Grand Café
- Cafe Nadi
- Dwiny

Hope these are indeed fun facts for you! Keep in touch. We would love to hear about your experiences, both in your search and during your actual Gap Year. You can email us at:info@aigya.org or visit our website at: www.aigya.org. And be sure to follow the ambassadors on Instagram: @israelgapyear.

Featured Resources

AMERICAN ISRAEL GAP YEAR ASSOCIATION (AIGYA)
https://www.americanisraelgapyearassociation.org/

AIGYA champions the cause of the Jewish continuity through the Israel Gap Year experience. We strive to be an objective and inclusive resource for families and educators to understand the breadth of Israel programs across the denominational spectrum. AIGYA feels that this transitional year in Israel is essential for students to take ownership of their Jewish identity and to solidify their relationship to Israel and the Jewish People.

What We Do

- Counseling, classes, and workshops to help students find their unique Gap Year experience.
- Program Directory available online in a multimedia format on our website www.aigya.org.
- Ambassador Program of specially selected students who chronicle their Gap Years in on social media on the AIGYA Instagram page for future students to explore a Gap Year in real time. @israelgapyear.
- Israel Gap Year Fair, the largest on the West Coast and the only cross-denominational Israel Fair in North America.
- The Rosina Korda Scholarships, awarded to three students each year.

To learn more about AIGYA go to www.aigya.org.

■ ■ ■

MASA ISRAEL JOURNEY
https://www.masaisrael.org/

Masa Israel Journey was founded in 2004 by the Prime Minister's Office of the Government of Israel, together with The Jewish Agency for Israel. They are the leader in immersive international experiences in Israel. "A Gap Year in Israel with us offers college-bound high school graduates the opportunity to acquire a global perspective and gain a taste of independent living, all while having an incredible Israel experience. Masa's transformational, authentic Israel experiences, among the best in the international experience space, empower participants to develop as individuals while also developing a robust global professional network that includes Israelis and Jews from around the world." Their program finder lets you search a range of dates, locations, and types of programs that includes internships and volunteer opportunities as well as Gap Year programs. They also help you navigate the practical details of the process. For more information, contact masainfo@masaisrael.org.

■ ■ ■

General Gap Year Resources

GAP YEAR ASSOCIATION
https://www.gapyearassociation.org/

Founded in 2012, the Gap Year Association is a public benefit not-for-profit Association with members. The GYA is recognized by the U.S. Department of Justice and the Federal Trade Commission as the Standards Development Organization for Gap Year education in the USA. Educators and families can use GYA resources for free to find quality Gap Year providers and Gap Year consultants, college deferral policies, financial aid, planning guides, and much more.

CANADA GAP YEAR ASSOCIATION
https://www.cangap.ca/

The Canadian Gap Year Association is a non-profit organization leading the Gap Year movement in Canada. With a mandate to support research, education and advocacy work, developing and curating resources for Gap Years, their goal is to elevate the Gap Year pathway for all Canadians.

. . .

To Read More About Taking a Gap Year

- *The Gap Year Advantage: Helping Your Child Benefit from Time Off Before or During College,* by Karl Haigler and Rae Nelson. Published in 2005 by St. Martin's Griffin.
- *The Complete Guide to the Gap Year: The Best Things to Do Between High School and College (2nd edition),* by Kristen White. Published in 2019 by Nota Bene Press.

. . .

Travel, Health, and Safety

All group programs in Israel require that students have family medical insurance and specific Israeli insurance policy associated with their program. Some also require a medical concierge service which provides students with health care professionals who can advocate at hospitals and clinics for emergencies and specific health issues.

***Centers for Disease Control and
Prevention's National Center for Infectious Diseases***
https://wwwnc.cdc.gov/travel

The Web site provides recommendations regarding immunizations, disease challenges, and other location-specific health information.

The US State Department
https://travel.state.gov/content/travel.html

This website provides updates on travel warnings regarding security, political instability, and health issues in countries and regions. The State Department's page for students (https://travel.state.gov/content/travel/en/international-travel/before-you-go/travelers-with-special-considerations/students.html) provides a Traveler's Checklist which includes information about passports and other required documents as well as how to contact the US. Embassy abroad.

The Israeli Consulate
https://embassies.gov.il/la/ConsularServices/Pages/Visa%20 Application.aspx

The Israeli Consulate is the official office of the Israeli government in the US Consular services includes issuing of visas, which are mandatory for any extended stay in Israel. Contact your regional office for visa application. Note: to receive a student visa you must submit a letter of approval from your educational institute. Masa Israel Journey (see below) can assist you in obtaining the necessary documents. The consulate or embassy has final jurisdiction with granting a visa, pending prior intelligence or concerns about a participant.

Masa Israel Journey
https://www.masaisrael.org/

More than any other Israel student travel organization, they have a wealth of up-to-the minute travel information about Visas, safety, and anything having to do with long-term student programming and travel. Masa students can receive approval for their educational institute or through the Masa program. To obtain a Masa Israel visa, you must visit a consulate or embassy with (1) The form you received from Masa Israel (PDF file) confirming your grant and/or scholarship amount; (2) A letter from your program organizer validating your acceptance to the program; (3) A valid passport obtained from the US Government. For questions contact masainfo@masaisrael.org.

Ema Care
https://www.healthcareisrael.com/about-us/ema-care

Ema Care provides case management and medical care services throughout Israel; their health care professionals, who speak English and Hebrew, help interface and navigate the Israeli health care system. They have a 24/7 Telemedicine service for students that offer advice, guidance, and physician referrals; if you have to go to the Emergency Room they will accompany and advocate.

■ ■ ■

Fundraising and Scholarships

For additional fundraising opportunities to the list below, consult the web sites for AIGYA and Gap Year Association.

AIGYA awards three Rosina Korda Israel Gap Year Scholarships annually to AIGYA program participants.

Masa Israel Journey provides grants and scholarships to help make the experience more affordable. Contact masainfo@masaisrael.org for more information. Funding is offered specifically for spending freshmen year in Israel, interning, volunteering, discovering your roots, and special interest programs in sports, high-tech and others.

International Association of Jewish Free Loans (IAJFL) IAJFL.org is an umbrella organization that offers interest-free loans through independently-run local agencies. Families can find and contact their home agency from this list: http://www.iajfl.org/for-borrowers/ and inquire about education loans, some of which have provisions for Gap Year activities.

International Hosteling USA
https://www.hiusa.org/

Offers a variety of scholarships for young US citizens wanting to travel for service learning and volunteer work.

Travel Access Project (scholarship money)
https://www.travelaccessproject.org/fund-a-scholarship

Awards Travel Access Gap Year Grants of up to $3,000 for ten students per year for individuals planning independent Gap Year experiences. Check the website for application dates and requirements.

■　■　■

To Get Involved and Learn More

Israel American Council
The mission of the Israeli-American Council (IAC) is to build an engaged and united Israeli-American community for the next

generation. They organize and activate through programming and activities to develop community leaders and establish strategic partnerships with a wide array of nonprofit organizations within the Jewish American community. Programming for teens includes:

- IAC Eitanim (www.israeliamerican.org/eitanim)
- ConnecTivism (www.israeliamerican.org/home/activism),
- Mishelanu (www.israeliamerican.org/mishelanu)
- Ofek (ofekhub.org/)

StandWithUs
https://www.standwithus.com/highschool

StandWithUs is a non-partisan Israel education organization, dedicated to supporting Israel and fighting antisemitism. The group works to empower a global network of high school and campus activists, has curriculum for middle school students, are leaders in social media, and has many resources that can help you educate yourself and your peers.

Email: highschool@standwithus.com
Number: T: 212-514-9200 ext. 3

Jewish National Fund
https://www.jnf.org/

Founded in 1901, the Jewish National Fund is a United Nations NGO. Involved in many aspects of nation building, including hospitals and roads, they are best known for planting trees in Israel and other agricultural initiatives. They offer several programs for students that include service vacations over winter break, an American semester abroad for high school students, tours, and a Gap Year program.

CHAPTER ONE: ISRAEL, JUDAISM, THE FUTURE, AND ME

1   https://www.facebook.com/692820428/posts/10158187284200429/?d=n.
2   Kelner, Shaul. *Tours that Bind: Diaspora, Pilgrimage, and Israeli Birthright Tourism.* New York University Press, 2010. Page 26.
3   https://www.pewforum.org/essay/american-and-israeli-jews-twin-portraits-from-pew-research-center-surveys/.
4   *"Lifting the Veil" Report on the Retrospective Study of Alumni: 2005–2014,* published 2015 by Rosov Consulting http://images.join.masaisrael.org/Web /MASA/%7B567b83f6-0836-4f8d-b4e2-63e0e9fc2809%7D_Masa_Alumni_ Study_Executive_Summary_-_November_2015_-_20160217.pdf.
5   Ibid.
6   https://www.hillel.org/jewish/leadership-engagement.
7   Chazan, Barry, Jewish Week staff, Josefin Dolsten, Phil Brown, Gary Levy, Hannah Dreyfus, Gary Rosenblatt, et al. "The Subject Of Israel Education Is Not Israel." Jewish Week, March 1, 2016. https://jewishweek.timesofisrael. com/the-subject-of-israel-education-is-not-israel/.

CHAPTER TWO: WHO AM I? WHAT INSPIRES ME?

8   https://www.gapyearassociation.org/data-benefits.php.

ACKNOWLEDGMENTS

To share what I know about the Gap Year and to see more students embrace this adventure in Israel is my mission in life. Books give things permanence and gravity; my hope is that the ideas I've generated will give students, families, and educators food for thought. By exploring the many wonderful programs described in this book, students should be that much closer to finding *their* right direction.

The Gap Year Advantage by Karl Haigler and Rae Nelson was one of the very first books about the Gap Year and became my Bible when I started Gap Year counseling. Their book helped me learn the tools needed to make this year successful for students. I am proud to say I got to know them both through my connection with the Gap Year Association. Rae became my book "angel," reading my chapters and offering thoughtful notes and encouragement.

Ethan Knight, the founder and Executive Director of the Gap Year Association, was the inspiration for my founding of the American Israel Gap Year Association (AIGYA). His professionalism, kindness, and generosity are only surpassed by his leadership in the field. The hard work of making the Gap Year the notable mission it is today rests firmly on his shoulders. He has been enormously helpful in all things Gap and personally supportive as a sounding board and friend.

This book really began with a cup of coffee with Joan Ziff, a woman who became my book muse. When I first shared my idea, she didn't just nod politely, she immediately set a date to help put my ideas on paper.

My other thought partner was, and is, the wonderfully calm and levelheaded Jean Horwatt, who always talked me down from any frustration, saw the positive, or helped me find a solution. Along the way, I received additional support from several community leaders and board members. Rebecca Coen, the former principal at a Los Angeles Jewish High school where I did independent counseling, let me run with my idea of creating an Israel Gap Fair at her school. This fair, which became AIGYA's calling card, grew to be the largest Israel Fair on the West Coast, and is the only cross-denominational Israel Fair in the US. Shira Hershoff, an Israel counselor, whose tireless work for her students, including helping my own daughters find the right Israel program, has always been someone I hope to emulate.

Rabbi Spodek and Rabbi Stulberger have been true champions of my cause and organization. Rabbi Stulberger, who is successful in sending his students at Valley Torah High School to Israel, shared my vision for the importance of bringing the Israel Gap Year to the collective Jewish community. He encouraged me to move forward on our very first meeting. An equally auspicious first meeting, which occurred with a 1:00 a.m. email introduction, was with Rabbi Spodek, the former head of YULA Girls School, who saw my mission as his own, and has been championing the cause ever since.

Board members Bruce Powell and Judy Levin have given invaluable advice and support on the "business" of non-profit work. Joanne Helperin has always offered her expertise for AIGYA's written communications. Thanks also to Ilanit Levanon, Linda Koffman, and Miriam Kosberg. Also, a special shout out to my assistant Dave Schwartz, whose quiet and dedicated aid has been enormously helpful throughout this book process. Thank you to designer Lilia Arbona, who is always there for me graphically. Thank you to Sara Stratton of Redwood Publishing for handling all the nuts and bolts.

Writers who I have turned to, or been inspired by, have offered me wisdom and help as I carved this narrative from my churning thoughts. Judy Gruen's sound advice about publishing was invaluable and Karen Propp, my talented developmental editor, was with me every step of the way. Erin Johnson, a post doc research fellow in sociology, whose projects include the intersection of learning, religion, and identity in the Jewish community, shared her thoughts as well as many articles on the subject of religion in general. Leann Gregory's work in the Christian Gap Year world was also the catalyst that gave me the freedom to say that one's faith is worth exploring. Religion, in general, is a fundamental moral compass; and Judaism and Israel are so specific to the sustainability of our peoplehood. A book dedicated to this exploration was not a frivolous exercise, but a worthwhile endeavor.

So many others on my AIGYA board, and my friends from the beginning of the organization, are worthy of thanks. Please read the list of supporters, sponsors, and tributes at the back of the book. Each person and organization, including my faith community the Westwood Kehilla, has been instrumental in their general support of AIGYA and me and could be inspirational to you.

Lastly, thanks go to my main benefactor in life, Mark Katchen. He has let me do what is most meaningful to me, which often meant that he had to work that much harder to provide for our family.

I once heard a gapper say that she didn't know who she would be when she returned from her Gap Year, but that was what was so exciting for her. The uncharted waters for the Gap Year was what excited her in shaping her future. This book represents my uncharted waters into the future—I hope that *Find Your Right Direction: The Israel Gap Year Guide* will be a tangible resource for more students to embark on this journey. That's what excites ME.

Generation Builders

As is fitting in a book about legacy and continuity, the following tributes honor individuals and their good works. We are specifically honoring these women of valor, men of distinction, those who have devoted themselves to supporting our youth, and the young people we look to for the future. They provide inspiration to all.

Women of Valor

In Honor of: Lauren Feinberg

Lauren, your enthusiasm and warmth brighten our
home and the lives of those around you. Thank
you for your selfless devotion to our family and
to the children of Gan and Bnos Aliya.

We love you,
Daniel, Emuna, Temima, Bruria, Margalit, Nessia, and Odelia

In Honor of: Julia Makowsky

Dearest Julia, after a long search, you are the best
thing that has happened to me. You are the most
amazing wife and mother. An inspiration to us all.

Shmuel

In honor of: Heather Kernoff

Heather Kernoff—A woman of enormous heart and the personification of kindness and generosity to all.

Gerald Kernoff, Jenny and Billie Gelb and Family

In Honor of: Jacalyn Saks Shalom

Dearest Jackie, you were born to help others. Our family and community are blessed to have received your kindness. May this message of praise make you a role-model to all who read this book.

Asher and Family

In Honor of: Miriam (Marissa) Proctor

Our mom's commitment to faith, her kindness and love has been our moral compass as we navigate the future. You are always on our minds and in our hearts.

Moshe Chaim, Avi and Tova Proctor

In Honor of: Jean Horwatt

To my wife Jean, the nicest person I've known, who has, on a daily basis, kept me from falling off life's emotional and spiritual tightrope since I was eighteen.

David Horwatt

In honor of: Norma Shippel

Normal Shippel, a woman of grace, elegance, wisdom and loving kindness, to us, her lucky children and grandchildren, to a world of dear friends and all who meet her.

The Shippel and Levitt Families

In honor of: Sheryl Katchen

Sheryl, you are so warm and caring and your devotion to Judaism is inspiring. Thank you for being such a dedicated wife, mother, daughter, and friend. We love and appreciate you.

Larry, Joshua, Sarah, Jenna, and Jonathan Katchen

In honor of: Phyllis Folb

In honor of Phyllis Folb who works tirelessly to ensure that all Jewish youth have the opportunity to fall in love with Israel.

From Shawni and Jeff Astroff

In Honor of: Gitty Meyers

To my Wonder Woman, Gitty. Many thanks for all
that you do from your loving and appreciative family.
~Mendel, Bina, Yitzchak, Chaiky, Izza, and Geulah

In Honor of: Tina Gall

Tina Gall, a woman of dignity, grace and compassion.
Thanks for being such a wonderful role model.
~Alexander Gall and Delara Aharpour, and Evan Gall

Men of Distinction

In Honor of: Stanley Folb

It is with fondness I pay tribute to my uncle Stanley Folb, the last of my father's siblings. The bible says remember the widowed and orphaned. He lived that by welcoming and taking care of my mother, and me, at sensitive times. He kept my father's memory alive for me and my entire family. For this, I am especially grateful. May his good deeds be recognized and remembered.
—Phyllis Folb

* * *

As Stanley Folb's eldest son, I have tried to follow in his footsteps, to help those who are less fortunate than us. Although his heart weighs heavily for all causes Jewish, he has always followed his heart to wherever he feels the need is greatest. He is an advocate for all humanity. I am honored to be his son.

I am so proud of my cousin Phyllis, daughter of my father's oldest brother, whom he loved and admired. Phyllis is a woman of strong conviction. Her beliefs and commitment to preserving our Jewish heritage are without compromise. This resource on the Israel Gap Year, an experience she holds dear, is her crowning moment. Congratulations Phyllis, in making this dream a reality.
—Brian Folb

In Honor of: Jack Nagel

Jack Nagel—A visionary at the forefront of both traditional and innovative Jewish educational models. He was a big believer in the Israel Gap Year and our mother, Gitta Nagel, continues to be. We are proud to honor him in this resource that supports this transformative year in Israel.

Marnie and David Nagel and The Nagel Family

Dor v dor (from Generation to Generation)

In Honor of: Max Levin

The year in Israel helped deepen his love
and devotion to the State of Israel.
During that year, he forged his own strong relationship
and bond with the people and the country. We are forever
grateful that there are such amazing Gap Year programs
available in Israel. Thank you Phyllis for all of your hard
work and efforts to make all of this available to our children.

Love, Judy and Bud Levin

In Honor of: Children of Klal Israel

Congratulations Phyllis Folb, our beloved friend, for dedicating
herself to the children of Klal Israel and Jewish continuity
through the Israel Gap Year. You are an inspiration!

The Westwood Kehilla

In Honor of: The Frankiel Generations

In honor of our amazing family of past and
future Israel gappers! Ilana, Adam, Liya, Coby,
Judith, Tani and Kess. We love you!!!

Mommy and Daddy (Marlene and Steve Frankiel)

COMMUNITY BUILDERS

Thank you to our sponsors and supporters who have recognized the importance of the Gap Year as a transformative experience. They represent the organizations, families, schools, synagogues, and individuals who believe that a Gap Year is a key to Jewish continuity. We could not do the work we do without their support.

Thank you to our Community Builders.

Rabbi Samuel S. and A. Irma Cohon Memorial Foundation
The Korda Family

∎ ∎ ∎

Barbara & Fred Kort Foundation
Masa Israel Journey

. . .

Brian Folb

Mark Katchen

. . .

Orna and David Delrahim

Stan Folb

Judy and Buddy Levin

Marnie and David Nagel

The Nagel Family

Debbie and Naty Saidoff

Batya Casper and Aryeh Zimmerman

. . .

Israel American Council

Jewish National Fund

StandWithUs

World Zionist Organization (Dpt of Edu)

Temple Aliyah

Beth Jacob Congregation

Beverly Hills Synagogue (YINBH)

B'nai David-Judea Congregation

Kehilat Yavneh

Sinai Temple

Westwood Kehilla

Young Israel Century City

de Toledo Community High School

Harkham GAON Academy

Shalhevet High School

Touro College LA

Valley Torah High School

YULA Boys High School

YULA Girls High School

NCSY

Shawni and Jeff Astroff

Lauren and Daniel Feinberg

Marlene and Steve Frankiel

Jean and David Horwatt

Heather and Gerald Kernoff

Julia and Shmuel Makowsky

Jacalyn and Asher Shalom

Laura and Mark Whitoff

■ ■ ■

Bnei Akiva of Los Angeles

Dorit and Shawn Evanheim

Jenny and Billie Gelb

Dick and Beverly Horowitz

Anne and Jonathan Levitt

Debbie and Bruce Powell

Phyllis and Rick Scott

Rabbi Yonason and Adina Shippel

■ ■ ■

Naomi Davis

Wendy and Clark Gross

Myrna and Herb Meyers

Gitty and Mendel Meyers

Harriet Reiter

Joanne Victor and Barry Steiner

Norma Shippel

Andrea and Greg Smith

■ ■ ■

Milken Community High School

Adat Shalom

Temple Beth Am

USY

World Union Progressive Judaism

ABOUT PHYLLIS FOLB

Since founding AIGYA in 2013, Phyllis Folb has dedicated herself to advocating for the Israel Gap Year as a post-secondary educational necessity. She herself has been called "the ultimate Israel Gap Year Program resource." Folb has previously published articles in *The Jerusalem Post* and the *Jewish Journal*, where she was a recipient of the Journal's "Mensch" honor. She is a sought after guest for TV, radio, and print. Phyllis is available to speak at conferences, events, and webinars on the topics of benefits of Gap Year programs, and the details of spending an Israel-based Gap Year. You can reach out to her by email at: pfolb@findyourrightdirection.com or pfolb@aigya.org

"My mission in life is to inspire students to take advantage of this extraordinary life-changing opportunity. I hope that this book and all the resources on our website will help you find your right direction.

"Wishing you a journey that propels you to new heights and provides you with insight, clarity, connection, and excitement as you go forward."

—*Phyllis Folb*

Made in the USA
Monee, IL
20 September 2020

42148489R00178